# AESTHETIC PERCEPTION

*A Thomistic Perspective*

KEVIN E. O'REILLY

FOUR COURTS PRESS

Set in 11 on 15 point AGaramond for
FOUR COURTS PRESS LTD
7 Malpas Street, Dublin 8, Ireland
e-mail: info@fourcourtspress.ie
http://www.fourcourtspress.ie
*and in North America by*
FOUR COURTS PRESS
c/o ISBS, 920 N.E. 58th Avenue, Suite 300, Portland, OR 97213.

ISBN 978-1-84682-027-4

A catalogue record for this title
is available from the British Library.

Printed in England
by Antony Rowe Ltd, Chippenham, Wilts.

# Contents

# Acknowledgments

I N BRINGING THIS BOOK to publication, I must necessarily thank those who have helped me in the course of my research. I would like to thank Br John Heneghan CFC for having allowed me to pursue my studies in philosophy. Although it has been completely revised, this work began as a doctoral thesis, firstly under the direction of Dr Dan Otten and then under that of the Revd Professor James McEvoy at the National University of Ireland, Maynooth. Dr Thomas A.F. Kelly, the present Acting Head of Philosophy at NUI Maynooth, was the internal reader and his suggestions proved to be valuable as, over a number of years, I reworked the manuscript. More recently, Dr Kelly has been kind enough to read the final manuscript, as has the Revd Dr Mark Sultana, Catholic University of Malta. Several years ago, Marcia L. Colish read and commented on an earlier version; her criticisms were incisive and forced me to rethink radically my application of the notion of knowledge through inclination to the realm of aesthetic perception. While I acknowledge the debt of gratitude I owe to those who have surveyed and commented upon my efforts, any flaws in this work naturally are to be attributed to me alone.

In recent times I have had the pleasure of working under Professor Santiago Sia, Dean of the Faculty of Philosophy at the Milltown Institute, Dublin. I thank him for his constant encouragement since his arrival at the Institute. I would also like to thank those friends who have been a constant support as I brought this work to completion, in particular to Pádraig Keogh, Pat, Kay, Mary and Lucia McCaughey, Fr Eugene McCaffrey ODC, and the Revd Dr Pat Gorevan. Finally, I wish to express my gratitude to my parents.

# Abbreviations

The following abbreviations of Aquinas' works are cited throughout the book. Publication details can be found in the bibliography. Also listed there are the English translations which I have consulted. Unless otherwise stated, I have employed these translations throughout. All translations from other languages are my own.

| | |
|---|---|
| ST | *Summa theologiae* |
| SCG | *Summa contra gentiles* |
| *Comm. Div. Nom. Nominibus* | *In librum beati Dionysii de Divinis* |
| *Comm. De Anima* | *In Aristotelis Librum De Anima* |
| *In Sent.* | *Scriptum super libros Sententiarum* |
| *De Veritate* | *Quaestiones disputatae de veritate* |
| *In Ethic.* | *Sententia libri Ethicorum* |
| *In Metaphys.* | *Expositio in libros Metaphysicorum* |
| *De potentia* | *Quaestiones disputatae de potentia* |

CHAPTER ONE

# Introduction

EXAMINATION OF THE SOURCES from which aesthetic theory is
derived leads to the conclusion that it is not an independent science,
but rather forms part of a general system of philosophy, borrowing its
principles from the primary branches – metaphysics and psychology.
Consequently, any complete philosophical synthesis must contain, at
least in embryo, the elements of a theory of beauty and art. Thus, for
example, even if Plato had never dealt with beauty in any of his dialogues
it would have been possible from an examination of his theory of ideas
to discern more than the outward form which a philosophy of the beautiful would assume in any system which drew its inspiration from him.
Again, neither Descartes nor Leibniz wrote directly on the subject; however, it is not difficult to construct either a Cartesian or a Leibnizian doctrine of the beautiful.

Although Aquinas did not leave behind a special tract on the theory
of beauty or art, reflections on both subjects are scattered throughout his
writings, being introduced wherever they are necessary or useful to the
development of some major thesis. In the *Summa Theologiae*, for instance,
his most mature work, we first encounter a discussion of the notion of
beauty in his treatment of the Divine Essence. Considering the nature
of goodness in general, Aquinas enquires whether goodness has the aspect
of a final cause. Among the objections adduced against his teaching is a
text from *De divinis nominibus* of the Pseudo-Dionysius, which seems
to imply the identity of the good and the beautiful. In offering his
solution to the objection Aquinas lays, in a few terse sentences, a solid
foundation for an aesthetic.[1] The same approach is found elsewhere in

1 'Beauty and goodness in a thing are identical fundamentally; for they are based upon
the same thing, namely, the form; and consequently *goodness is praised as beauty*. However,
they differ logically. For good (being *what all things desire*) has to do properly with desire

II

the *Summa* in relation to the subject of beauty: whenever it is discussed, it is by way of explanation of something else, and it is always secondary and subordinate to some more prominent subject.[2] The other aspect of aesthetic experience, artistic production, is treated in the same manner – 'succinctly but profoundly'.[3] Aquinas did not expound a doctrine of the beautiful in the same way as he dealt with topics such as logic, metaphysics and ethics; nevertheless, what he does say on the subject opens up immense horizons of thought and contains a whole aesthetic theory in embryo.

Interest in aesthetic theory does not seem to have figured prominently among the Scholastic successors of Aquinas. It was only with the revival of Scholasticism in the latter half of the nineteenth century that attempts were made to propound a theory in accordance with Thomistic principles. An important influence was Jacques Maritain, whose major relevant contributions were *Art and Scholasticism*[4] and *Creative intuition in art and poetry*.[5] In the words of Umberto Eco, 'it is to Maritain that we owe the reinstatement of medieval aesthetics as a living force in contemporary thought, and this is no small debt'.[6]

## *Maritain's* Art and Scholasticism, *historiography and the aesthetic* visio[7]

*Art and Scholasticism* was the work of a self-professed disciple of Aquinas. In this work, Maritain attempted to deal with the problems posed by

and so involves the idea of an end (since desire is a kind of movement towards something). Beauty, on the other hand, has to do with knowledge, for those things are called beautiful which please us when they are seen. This is why beauty is a matter of right proportion, for the senses delight in rightly-proportioned things as similar to themselves, the sense-faculty being a sort of proportion itself, like all other knowing faculties. Now since knowing proceeds by imaging, and images have to do with form, beauty properly involves the notion of formal causes': ST, 1, 5, 4 ad 1. The translation of this passage offered here differs slightly from that in the Blackfriars edition of the *Summa Theologiae*. **2** See ST, 1–2, 27, 1 ad 3; 2–2, 145, 2. **3** L. Callahan, *A theory of aesthetics according to the principles of St Thomas of Aquino* (Washington, 1927), p. 20. **4** Trans. by J. F. Scanlan (London, 1930). **5** New York, 1953. **6** *Art and beauty in the Middle Ages*, trans. by Hugh Bredin (London, 1986), p. 28. **7** The term *visio* is the abstract noun corresponding to

modern art, offering contemporary culture the treasures of a medieval aesthetic previously unknown to it. Not surprisingly the culture of the thirties, being largely unfamiliar with the Scholastic philosophical and theological tradition, received these suggestions as novelties. Maritain spoke, for instance, of art as *recta ratio factibilium* (a right manner of making things) which disposes materials according to an order dictated not only by sensibility, but primarily by intelligence; and of beauty as a synthesis of three formal criteria, namely proportion, integrity and clarity.

Maritain's thought, it ought to be pointed out, was animated by a strong speculative impulse. In the case of aesthetic theory, he attempted to deal in a Thomistic vein with issues of contemporary relevance, issues which were not of concern to the medievals and so were not dealt with by Aquinas himself. Eco argued that it was precisely through Maritain's efforts to address the problems posed by modern art that the latter ended up by substituting his own thinking for that of Aquinas and, in so doing, conflating speculative philosophy with the historiography of medieval thought. Maritain would doubtless have objected to this contention: he felt he was developing Thomism, not substituting his own thought for that of Aquinas. According to Eco, however, Maritain had absolutely no interest in historiography; this resulted in what Eco considered to be 'violent interpretations'[8] of Aquinas.

As an illustration Eco cites Maritain's definition of beauty as 'what gives pleasure on sight, *id quod visum placet*'.[9] This definition is very popular with neo-Thomists, many of whom believe it to be a quotation from Aquinas. What Aquinas actually states is *pulchra enim dicuntur quae visa placent*, that is to say, 'those things are called beautiful which please when they are seen'.[10] The difference between the two definitions is, according to Eco, considerable: Aquinas' refers to what Eco calls a 'soci-

---

the verb *videre*, which means 'to see'. The past participle of this verb (*visa*, meaning 'seen'), appears of course in Aquinas' statement that 'those things are called beautiful which please when they are seen'. When we speak of the aesthetic *visio*, we are therefore referring to aesthetic perception. I choose to employ the term *visio*, however, since it is unavoidable in arguments which I put forward at a later stage. In this way a greater consistency in the use of language is achieved. **8** *La definizione dell'arte* (Milan, 1968), p. 105. **9** Maritain, *Art and Scholasticism*, p. 23. **10** ST, I, 5, 4 ad 1.

ological fact', whereas Maritain's amounts to a 'metaphysical definition'.[11] Eco accepts that it would be a little harsh to accuse Maritain of falsehood here, for Maritain is trying to construct a synthesis out of more than one Thomistic formula. Nevertheless, as Eco points out, he is not totally innocent, for his definition (*id quod visum placet*) is actually presented in *Art and Scholasticism* as a quotation.

Eco also contends that the greater metaphysical incisiveness of Maritain's definition enables him to identify the aesthetic *visio* with an intuitive act possessing a certain contemporary character. In so doing, Maritain is well aware that for Aquinas the human intellect is not intuitive in the way in which angelic intellects are and that 'nothing is in the intellect which was not first in the senses'. In his desire to explain the function of the intellect in aesthetic experience Maritain argues therefore that the intellect comes into contact with beauty only through the senses, because only these possess the capacity for intuition which is required for perceiving beauty. Beauty is apprehended '*in the sensible and by the sensible*, and not separately from it'.[12] The intellect does not exercise its powers of abstraction, since it does not have to extricate anything from the matter in which it is buried and then examine step by step the various attributes of what it has extricated. It rejoices, rather, 'without labour and without discussion' as it 'drinks the clarity of being'.[13] The aesthetic moment thus interpreted is in the words of Eco 'contemplative, uncritical, blessed'.[14]

Eco considers the notion of poetic knowledge as knowledge *through connaturality* to be a modern form of intuitionism. It is not difficult, in his view, to see how this notion, taken up at greater length by Maritain in later works, can be traced back to his understanding of the aesthetic *visio* as its source. Eco describes this understanding of the aesthetic *visio* as 'a first sign … of a forcing of Thomism in other directions, a confirmation of that systematic and most forceful violence to texts which was constantly taking place in this little book'.[15]

---

**11** Eco, *The aesthetics of Thomas Aquinas*, trans. by Hugh Bredin (Cambridge, 1988), p. 240 n. 22. **12** *Art and Scholasticism*, p. 25. **13** Ibid., p. 26. **14** Eco, *Aesthetics*, p. 60. **15** *La definizione*, p. 106.

The most mature statement of Maritain's aesthetic theory is found in his celebrated *Creative Intuition in Art and Poetry*, where he argues that poetic or artistic knowledge is a specific form of knowledge through connaturality or inclination. This notion, referring to a nonconceptual kind of knowledge, is borrowed directly from Aquinas. Aquinas employs the notion of knowledge through connaturality primarily in speaking of mystical experience. To elucidate the specific character of mystical experience, Aquinas provides a natural analogue from the realm of morality. Never, in contrast, does he employ the notion of knowledge through connaturality in what he has to say about beauty or art. The question arises therefore as to whether Maritain's theory of intuition is faithful to the Thomistic philosophical principles which he openly espouses, or whether it is historiographically suspect as Eco would have us believe – a theory in which Thomistic influences are merely 'a lesson from history which is assimilated freely'.[16]

## Human nature and the aesthetic visio

Although it is our belief that Maritain is innocent of the charges levelled against him by Eco, our exoneration of him is not the final goal of this work. In excavating the concept of knowledge through connaturality, Maritain could be said to have initiated a process which has led gradually to a liberation of Aquinas from the distortions which interpretation through the lens of Enlightenment rationalism wreaked on the latter's thought, particularly his philosophy of mind.

While the force of reason is powerful, at times perhaps almost overwhelming, in Aquinas, he nonetheless is not an intellectualist. Notions of objectivity of course reign supreme, as does the idea that truth claims have a universal extension and validity. Nevertheless, Aquinas' thought is not characterised by the violence which at times enters into the discourse of rationalism. (Hegel is of course the epitome of such violence, but its roots are to be found in Kant and, ultimately, in Descartes.) The

16 Eco, *Art and beauty*, p. 128.

reason for this is perhaps because Aquinas' understanding of human nature is arguably far richer than that of any later writer. Not only does he offer an account of a whole array of aspects of human nature, this account is also supremely integrated and is sensitive to the dynamic interplay between reason, the emotions, and our bodies in a way which is perhaps unequalled in this history of Western thought.

Unfortunately, interpretations of Aquinas' embryonic theory of aesthetic perception have to date failed to take into consideration his understanding of human nature as an integrated unity and its implications for the life of mind. As a result, they have fallen foul of the Kantian notion that such a thing as 'pure' reason actually exists, a notion which Hans-Georg Gadamer has in recent times debunked.[17] Arguably the most influential among the interpretations of Aquinas' embryonic aesthetic theory is Eco's fine exegetical study, *The Aestethics of Thomas Aquinas*. While Eco clarifies the intellectual processes leading to the act of judgement which is required for any human experience of beauty, his approach is nonetheless seriously defective in that it fails to appreciate sufficiently the implications of what is the most important principle underlying Aquinas' account of human nature: humans are unitary composite beings. What we mean by this expression is that Aquinas refuses to compartmentalise the various aspects of human nature. Thus, for example, while he certainly isolates and considers the workings of the intellect, on the one hand, and the life of the emotions, on the other, his texts underline the dynamic interplay between reason and the emotions. The following observation from Martha Nussbaum would receive approbation from Aquinas: 'Emotions are not just the fuel that powers the psychological mechanism of a reasoning creature, they are parts, highly complex and messy parts, of this creature's reasoning itself.'[18]

It is our aim in this speculative engagement with Aquinas' thought to develop a few reflections on the nature of aesthetic perception on the

---

17 Hans-Georg Gadamer, *Truth and method* (London, 2004). 18 Martha C. Nussbaum, *Upheavals of thought: the intelligence of emotions* (Cambridge, 2001), p. 3. It must be admitted nevertheless that Aquinas' conception of the precise nature of the relationship obtaining between reason and emotion differs from that of Nussbaum.

basis of his unitary understanding of human nature. In other words, we wish to work out some of the implications of the dynamic interplay between reason, emotion and the body for our response to and appreciation of objects of beauty. As our work progresses, the insight of Hans-Georg Gadamer that there is no such thing as 'pure' reason will come to the fore precisely on the basis of this dynamic interplay between reason, emotion and body. This notion, however, is not a novel one in the history of Western thought; as we will see, it forms an integral part of Aquinas' intellectual edifice, although it is not made explicit.

According to Gadamer, all understanding inevitably involves some prejudice. Reacting against the fundamental prejudice of the Enlightenment, namely 'the prejudice against prejudice itself, which denies tradition of its power', Gadamer argues that there are 'such things as préjugés légitimes',[19] legitimate prejudices which are transmitted by authority properly understood. It is clear that for Aquinas, as ought to be the case for any Christian, the most important 'préjugé légitime', that which provides the ultimate conditions for epistemic objectivity, is faith – that theological virtue which perfects the intellect – taken in conjunction with charity and hope. What the implications of prejudices, and in particular the legitimate prejudice of faith, are for the perception and appreciation of beautiful objects will be the subject of reflection in chapters six and seven, where we will offer a speculative working-out of the notion of knowledge through inclination drawn from Aquinas' virtue ethics. Hence our reflections will necessarily be theological as well as philosophical.

Before we can offer these reflections, we must first of all lay the necessary foundations. In doing so, we will draw principally upon Umberto Eco's exegesis of Aquinas' embryonic aesthetic theory, Jacques Maritain's speculative development of this theory with regard to artistic creativity, and Rafael-Tomás Caldera's exegesis of Aquinas' notion of knowledge through connaturality/inclination. In the first instance, we will turn to Aquinas' embryonic aesthetic theory.

---

**19** Gadamer, *Truth and method*, 273.

CHAPTER TWO

# The formal constitutive elements of beauty

THE IDENTIFICATION OF THE formal constitutive elements of
beauty – proportion (*proportio*), integrity (*integritas*) and clarity
(*claritas*) – constitutes one of the best-known aspects of Aquinas' aesthetic theory. To clarify the meaning which he attached to these elements,
I now propose to examine his own words in the context of his thought
as a whole. Much of what I have to say in this regard is based on Umberto
Eco's exposition of these elements in his treatment of Aquinas' aesthetic
theory.[1]

The simplest texts that mention the three constitutive elements of
beauty occur in the *Summa Theologiae*. One such reference is found at
ST, I, 5, 4 ad 1. Aquinas asserts that beauty pertains to knowledge (*vis
cognoscitiva*), so that 'those things are called beautiful which please us
when they are seen'. He then says that 'this is why beauty is a matter of
right proportion, for the senses delight in rightly proportioned things as
similar to themselves, the sense-faculty being a sort of proportion itself
like all other knowing faculties'. In this passage proportion is singled out
for mention.

The three formal criteria of beauty are systematically formulated only
once in the *Summa Theologiae*, in the context of a discussion of the essential attributes assigned to the Persons of the Trinity. Here Aquinas states
that 'beauty must include three qualities: integrity or completeness –
since things that lack something are thereby ugly; right proportion or
harmony; and brightness – we call things bright in color beautiful'.[2]

Eco believes that the only place where Aquinas employs the term
*integritas* to refer specifically to the formal character of beauty is in the
passage just quoted. Cyril Barrett, however, argues that although Aquinas

1 See *Aesthetics*, pp 64–121, for a more detailed discussion.  2 ST, I, 39, 8.

does not refer to *integritas* by name, he clearly has it in mind as the third of the three elements of beauty that he cites in his *Commentary on the Sentences*.³ Aquinas traces the source of 'consonance and clarity' to Dionysius, while observing that Aristotle 'adds a third when he says that beauty is found only in a large body; thus small men can be called correctly proportioned and well shaped, but not beautiful'.⁴ So, although Aquinas rarely mentions the Aristotelian element again until the familiar passage in the *Summa Theologiae, integritas* is a notion which goes back to his early career.

Aquinas refers again to consonance and clarity in his commentary on the *De Divinis Nominibus* of the Pseudo-Dionysius where he avers that 'God confers beauty on things in that he is the cause of consonance and clarity in everything. So we say a man is beautiful on account of his well-proportioned dimensions and surroundings, and because of his clear and bright complexion'.⁵

Having cited the main passages in which proportion, integrity, and clarity are mentioned, it is now necessary to examine each of these elements individually in the context of Aquinas' thought as a whole to elucidate them further.

## Proportio

In the *Summa contra Gentiles* 3, 54, 13, when discussing how we will see God, Aquinas refers to proportion as *habitudo*, meaning a relation of one thing to another. One instance is the relation of matter to form. It is clear that for Aquinas proportion signifies the suitability of matter for the reception of form. Matter is in potency to the form that actualizes and orders it, and matter and form are mutually adapted and integrated.⁶ In a similar way SCG 2, 16, 8 calls attention to the proportion obtaining between a matter and its action: an agent with a certain kind of power must have a matter proportioned to that power; for example, a man with the power

<hr>

**3** See Cyril Barrett, 'The aesthetics of St Thomas re-examined,' *Philosophical Studies* 12 (1963) 110. **4** *1 Sent.* d. 31, q. 2, a. 1, sol. **5** *Comm. Div. Nom.,* 4, 5. **6** See SCG, 2, 80–1, 7.

of vision must have eyes. Here proportion is conceived of as a process: the action of any non-divine agent upon matter is described as a progressive movement in which matter gives itself up to order and form.

A second kind of proportion is that which obtains between essence and existence. A thing has proportion precisely because it exists, because it 'is'. A thing 'is' when its essence is complemented by existence, and this entails a proportion. Since proportion is constitutive of beauty, we can say that everything is beautiful in so far as it 'is'. In the words of Eco, 'something is beautiful in so far as it "is," and it "is" in so far as it is beautiful; and it has beauty in that it has proportion'.[7]

A further kind of proportion is the adequacy of a thing to what it is supposed to be, that is to say, to its form. Alternatively, proportion can also signify the harmony between an object and its function. Indeed, these two types of adequacy are closely connected, because when an object is what it ought to be it is also proportioned to its function – for function is the perfection or completion of form.[8]

Proportion, as well as referring to sensible relations, can also signify a purely rational concordance between things. Hence a sequence of thought, in so far as it conforms to the laws of thought, is well-proportioned. Then there is also moral proportion, encountered in the relation of morally upright actions and thoughts to the practical dictates of natural reason or to the dictates of the divine law. Thus, writes Aquinas, 'beauty of spirit consists in conversation and actions that are well-formed and suffused with intelligence'.[9]

Having considered some of the many ontological aspects of proportion, let us now turn our attention to some of its psychological aspects. Edgar de Bruyne notes that Aquinas was alone among his contemporaries in drawing a distinction between psychological proportion and ontological proportion.[10] An example of such a relation is the compatibility of a sense organ with a given sensible quality, for 'the senses delight in rightly proportioned things as similar to themselves, the sense-faculty being a sort of proportion like all other knowing faculties'.[11] Sight is com-

---

7 Eco, *Aesthetics*, 85. **8** See ST, 1, 73, 1. **9** ST, 2–2, 145, 2. **10** *Études d'esthétique mediévale*, vol. 3 (Bruges, 1946), p. 302. **11** ST, 1, 5, 4 ad 1.

patible with colour, for instance; hearing with sound; and so on. Objectively rule-governed qualities can exist in sensible phenomena, as when sounds are combined to create a melody, for example, or when colours are juxtaposed in a painting. When the human senses are faced with such phenomena they display an ability to grasp their *ratio* or logic – in other words, their proportion.

Aquinas explains this idea more fully in his commentary on Aristotle's *De Anima*, arguing that, since every harmonious sound is somehow identical with the faculty of hearing, 'the fact that the sound is a kind of harmony implies that hearing is the same'.[12] Indeed, just after the passage quoted from the *Summa*, Aquinas talks of the corruption of the senses by an excess of sensation: such excess destroys their mutual harmony.

Eco points out that in addition to this proportion of the senses to their object, there is the proportion between the intellect and its object. Aquinas refers to this early on in the *Summa Theologiae* when he asks whether it is possible for a created mind to see the essence of God.[13] He says that there is a cognitive relation between the human intellect and the divine essence on account of the 'proportion' which exists between them. This proportion has its basis in the fact that creatures are related to God 'as effects to a cause and as the partially realized to the absolutely real'.[14] However, divine light is necessary for this kind of cognition, for the divine completely transcends the intellect's capacity to know.[15]

It is reasonable to conclude from the foregoing account that in Aquinas' view there is a certain relationship between the psychological dispositions of the perceiver and the nature of the act of perceiving. De Bruyne captures this relationship in the following words:

> The mind does not project its own harmony into things and does not create beauty. It does not passively receive the objective harmony of form and does not suffer beauty. It recognizes the pre-

---

**12** *Comm. De Anima*, 3, 2, 597. **13** ST, I, 12, I. **14** ST, I, 12, I ad 4. **15** Several commentators have emphasised this psychological type of proportion. Bernard Bosanquet, for instance, perceives Plotinian influences in the notion of proportion and concludes: 'The ultimate ground of attraction in beauty is the affinity, revealed in symmetry, between the percipient and the perceived' (London, 1904), p. 147.

established harmony obtaining between the structure of the subject and that of the object and finds itself bathing in a world that
is completely musical. That is what brings about aesthetic delight.[16]

Eco opines that, in general, psychological proportion primarily *allows* the
aesthetic act, whereas ontological proportion is the *ground* of the causes
of aesthetic pleasure.[17] Each is a necessary (but insufficient) condition for
the actualization of beauty. Both together are the sufficient condition.

## Integritas

Another characteristic attributed by Aquinas to beauty is wholeness or
perfection (*integritas sive perfectio*). In discussing the various types of proportion mentioned above, I mentioned the adequacy of a thing to itself,
that is to say, a thing's adequacy to the requirements of its form. Aquinas
equates integrity with perfection. Thus he writes: 'The first type of perfection is present when the thing has all that makes up its substance. The
whole object's form is its perfection and arises out of the integrity of its
parts.'[18] A thing is adequate to itself only when nothing of what its form
requires is missing. Étienne Gilson expresses this point well: 'By deter-
mining its type, form also determines the conditions required for the
integrity of any being.'[19] Aquinas writes: 'Things that lack something are
thereby ugly.'[20] For a thing to be beautiful, therefore, it must have all
that is required of it by its nature, otherwise it suffers at least a diminu-
tion of its beauty.

On these grounds, Eco argues that integrity is a kind of proportion.[21]
The notion of integrity is clearly implied by Aquinas when he posits that
'there are two kinds of deformity in the human body. One arises from a
defect in some limb, so that we call mutilated people ugly. What they lack
is a due proportion [of parts] to the whole.'[22] It seems reasonable to claim
that if a certain proportion is demanded by the nature of a thing, then this
proportion is something which that thing should not lack. Hence propor-

16 *Études*, p. 302.  17 *Aesthetics*, p. 95.  18 ST, i, 73, 1.  19 *The arts of the beautiful* (New York,
1965), p. 30.  20 ST, i, 39, 8.  21 *Aesthetics*, p. 99.  22 *In IV Sent.*, d. 44, q. 3, a. 1, sol. 1.

tion is subsumed under the notion of integrity. On the other hand, if an object is to be duly proportioned it must have everything required by its nature. In this case the notion of integrity comes under that of proportion. It is evident therefore that proportion and integrity are mutually implicative notions. However, the fact that they are mutually implicative does not prevent them from being logically distinct.[23]

In his commentary on the *De Anima*, Aquinas argues that everything 'has certain limits to its size and increase'. Thus 'men are not all equal in size. But there is a limit both to their largeness and to their littleness.'[24] According to Eco, these remarks imply that integrity may be impaired by default or excess. In support of his interpretation he appeals to Aquinas' assertion that the forms of things are similar to numbers in that any change, that is to say, any addition or subtraction, interferes with the nature of the species and transmutes the species into a different one.[25]

Eco states that aesthetic experience of a thing is governed by the concept of the thing; it involves a judgment concerning the degree of conformity between the thing and its concept.[26] To the extent that a particular thing and its concept do not agree, to that extent is aesthetic judgment vitiated. Thus the concept of bodily integrity means that a mutilated body evokes a negative aesthetic appraisal.

As our study progresses, however, it will become clear that one can find resources in Aquinas' thought which support the contention that

23 The notions of proportion and integrity and an appreciation of their dynamic interplay in the appreciation of works of art can perhaps be discerned in the aesthetic speculations of John Dewey. Dewey tells us that the elucidatory-critical understanding of the arts is analytic and synthetic, that is to say, it moves back and forth between attention to discrete elements and to their relation to the whole (John Dewey, *Art as experience*, New York, 1934, p. 313). We could say that this dynamic movement between parts and whole facilitates an ever-deepening appreciation of the work of art. Indeed, for an appreciation of its formal constitution this movement is indispensable.

The relationship of mutual ordering to each other of proportion and integrity is brought out by Arnold Isenberg who has pointed out that similar elements can function very differently in different works. Thus, while a falling wavelike contour may be graceful in one painting, in another it is jarring. A modulation in one piece of music may be stimulating; in another it might well be gaudy. All depends on the relationship between part and whole: Arnold Isenberg, 'Critical communication', *Philosophical Review* 57 (1949), 330–44. 24 *Comm. De Anima*, 2, 8, 332. 25 ST, 1–2, 52, 1. 26 *Aesthetics*, p. 101.

experience of beauty is constituted by more than an apprehension of an object mediated by pure concepts. Just as Alasadair MacIntyre observes that 'observance of the laws of logic is only a necessary and not a sufficient condition for rationality, whether theoretical or practical',[27] so too one might make the same claim with regard to concepts, for they are always embedded in and determined by a particular tradition with its values and constructs. There are resources in Aquinas' body of thought which, for example, enable us to acknowledge that artworks mediate worldviews with their attendant clusters of values and that they communicate something of the inner life of the artist himself. Thus, while Eco's exegesis of Aquinas' understanding is correct in so far as it goes, the problem is that it does not go far enough. The horizons of the former's exegesis is restricted by the lens of Enlightenment rationalism which unwittingly comes to bear on his work.

## Claritas

We have glimpsed how extremely rich the notion of proportion is. However, for all that form possesses proportion in itself and is proportionately related to us, the problem arises as to how we are to perceive it. Eco raises the question as to whether it is the attitude of the experiencing subject with regard to the object that gives rise to the impression of order, or whether instead order is an ontological property of form.[28] The notion of *claritas* is the key to the solution of this problem.

For Aquinas, the form of things is not only that by means of which they possess being; it is also the cause of their beauty: 'Beauty properly involves the notion of formal causes.'[29] Beauty can be said to be a property of form, since a 'property' is a necessary consequence of form. Clarity is also a property of form, for all form participates in the divine clarity.[30] Thus, either both beauty and clarity are the same property or they are correlative properties. I will argue, following Eco, that clarity is the capacity which a form possesses to communicate itself, but which is only actu-

27 Alasdair MacIntyre, *Whose justice? Which rationality?* (Notre Dame, IN, 2003), p. 4.
28 *Aesthetics*, p. 102.   29 ST, 1, 5, 4 ad 1.   30 *Comm. Div. Nom.*, 4, 5.

alised by someone's looking at or 'seeing' the object. In other words, beauty results from the interaction between subject and object, between the subject's aesthetic *visio* and the object's *claritas*.

Aquinas' theory of sense perception bears out this contention. According to this theory there are no intermediaries between the perceiver and what is perceived. In sensation the sense-faculty does not come into contact with a mere likeness of the sense-object's form; rather, it becomes 'like' the sense-object by taking on the sense-object's form. This it does however in an intentional, not in a physical, manner. Aquinas expresses his theory of sense-perception very succinctly with a slogan borrowed from Aristotle: the sense-faculty which is actualised is the same as the sense-object which is actualised (*sensus in actu est sensibile in actu*).[31] To illustrate this claim let us take an example relating to the faculty of taste – the sweetness of a piece of sugar. The sweetness is a sense-object; the ability to taste is a sense-faculty. Now the sugar's tasting sweet to the one who tastes it is the same as his tasting the sweetness of the sugar. In other words, the actuality of the sense of taste in regard to the sensible object is the same as the actuality of the sensible object in relation to the sense of taste. Although sugar is always actually sweet, it tastes sweet only potentially until such time as it is placed in the mouth of a subject.

Just as Aquinas' theory of intentionality maintains an identity between the actualisation of the sense-faculty and the actualisation of a sensible object, so it also maintains that the actualisation of the capacity for thinking is the same thing as the actualisation of an object of thought: *intellectus in actu est intellectum in actu*.[32] This is because on the one hand the intellect is simply the capacity for thought – it possesses no structure or matter – while on the other hand the object of intellectual thought, a universal as such, is something which enjoys no existence outside of thought.

In the light of this principle, clarity can be said to be the capacity of form to communicate itself, a capacity which is made actual only in by someone's 'seeing' the object. One could express this idea with this slogan: the actualisation of an object's clarity is identical with the actualisation of an act of 'seeing': *visio in actu est claritas in actu*. This formula serves

31 ST, I, 87, 1 ad 3.  32 Ibid.

to bring out Aquinas' stance *vis-à-vis* the beautiful, a stance which in the words of Cyril Barrett 'avoids the twofold error of giving beauty an absolute objective status, on the one hand, and of making it a mere projection or objectification of a subjective experience, on the other'.[33]

This interpretation implies that any discussion of beauty should not only pay due attention to beauty's double aspect (subjective and objective), but should also seek to elucidate the dynamic interrelationship obtaining between them. In other words, any account of beauty should explain the identity which obtains between the subject's aesthetic *visio* and the object's *claritas*.[34] This reading also implies, that rational endeavour enables a person to deepen his experience of an aesthetic artifact. The notion that intellectual analysis destroys aesthetic experience must be rejected as having no place in Thomistic aesthetic theory.

Before proceeding to a consideration of the foundations of Aquinas' understanding of the aesthetic *visio* in his philosophy of mind, we propose to appraise the value of Maritain's definition of beauty as 'what gives pleasure on sight, *id quod visum placet*',[35] a definition which in Eco's estimation gives rise to a distinctive theory of artistic creativity, one which conflates Thomism and Bergsonism. In dealing with the issue of this definition's fidelity to Aquinas' own statements concerning beauty we can also avail ourselves of the opportunity to deepen further our own understanding of the metaphysical status of beauty in his thought.

## Maritain's 'id quod visum placet' *re-examined*

It is evident from the foregoing discussion that beauty is rooted in form. (We will of course argue later on that apprehension of this form is not by 'pure' reason; at this juncture, however, we leave aside this point to concentrate on formal beauty.) Proportion, integrity and clarity are three ways in which form can be considered *as a whole*. Each of these three elements necessarily implies the other two. In the words of Umberto Eco:

---

**33** 'The aesthetics of St Thomas', 110.  **34** For a further development of the notion *visio in actu est claritas in actu*, see chapter 3, pp 37–9.  **35** *Art and Scholasticism*, p. 23.

Form is proportion with integrity which manifests itself as such; form is the totality of a relation as it manifests itself; form is the self-signifying proportion of some whole. The three criteria are reciprocally implicative, each continually referring to the other, and no description of any one of them can be allowed to obscure the reality of the other two. The reality of form is the permanent substratum of this interplay of references.[36]

Proportion, integrity and clarity are therefore mutually implicative notions. In this 'interplay of references', clarity signifies the capacity of form to communicate itself. However, this capacity can be actualised only by someone's 'seeing' the object in question. If we ask what it is that *claritas* communicates, we must reply that it communicates the beauty of an object, since beauty pertains to formal causes. We know that for Aquinas beautiful things are those which when seen give pleasure. Thus, what *claritas* communicates when actualised is the object's beauty; what the aesthetic *visio* apprehends when it actualises the capacity of the object's form to communicate itself – its *claritas* – is the beauty of the object. We know that in sensible apprehension an identity is established between the sense-faculty and a sense-object: *sensus in actu est sensibile in actu*. The same principle is at work in intellectual apprehension: *intellectus in actu est intellectum in actu*. A similar identity is operative in aesthetic experience: *visio in actu est claritas in actu*.

It becomes clear therefore that Maritain's definition of beauty as 'what gives pleasure on sight, *id quod visum placet*', is in fact a legitimate development of Aquinas' thought. It is far from being an illicit speculative development of his definition of beautiful things – as those which when seen give pleasure – into a metaphysical definition. Indeed the charge of violent interpretations[37] of Aquinas' thought that Eco levels against Maritain is not only excessive, but it turns out upon examination to have no foundation whatsoever. The legitimacy of Maritain's speculative development appears to be indicated by Aquinas himself when he states that 'Beauty ... has to do with knowledge, for those things are called beautiful which please

36 *Aesthetics*, p. 121.  37 *La definizione*, p. 105.

us when they are seen'. In this single sentence we find reference both to beauty and to beautiful things, to *pulchrum* and to *pulchra*.[38] The second half of the sentence is in fact really an explication of the first half: beauty has to do with knowledge. What does that mean? It means that the intellect must first apprehend a beautiful object before the will can delight in its beauty: beautiful things are those which when seen afford pleasure.

The purpose of ST, I, 5, 4 is to ascertain whether goodness has the aspect of a final cause. *Objectio* I argues that it does not because as Dionysius says, 'goodness is praised as beauty', and beauty has the aspect of a formal cause. Goodness therefore also has the aspect of a formal cause. It is interesting that in this *objectio* and in the corresponding *responsio*, the word *pulchrum* occurs seven times; this contrasts with the incidence of the word *pulchra*, which we encounter only once. This does suggest very strongly that in so far as aesthetic matters are concerned, Aquinas' attention is focused on beauty rather than on beautiful things, on *pulchrum* rather than on *pulchra*.

Moreover the aim of the response is to distinguish between goodness and beauty, between *bonum* and *pulchrum*. According to Aquinas they are based on the same thing – form; that is why goodness is praised as beauty. However, they differ logically, 'for good (being *what all things desire*) has properly to do with desire and so involves the idea of an end (since desire is a kind of movement towards something). Beauty, on the other hand, has to do with knowledge, for those things are called beautiful which please us when they are seen.'[39] The second part of the final sentence is offered by Aquinas simply as a terse explication of the first. Both are pithy statements of how beauty differs from goodness: it does so by virtue of its reference to the cognitive faculty.

We know from our examination of the three formal constitutive elements of beauty that form is their natural foundation, both ontologically and psychologically. Aquinas himself points out that 'since knowing proceeds by imaging, and images have to do with form, beauty properly involves the notion of formal causes'.[40] Form is a fundamental concept

---

**38** '[P]ulchrum autem resicit vim cognoscitivam, pulchra enim dicuntur quae visa placent'. **39** ST, I, 5, 4 ad I.

in all Aquinas' statements pertaining to aesthetic matters: the objective foundation of beauty is located in the formal structure of objects. Moreover beauty (although it is not in our estimation a transcendental property of being properly speaking) is nonetheless coextensive with being itself.[41] This is because it is a function of both truth and goodness and is coterminous with them. Indeed, as we know, a thing's proportion is a consequence of its existence: a thing has proportion precisely because it exists, precisely because it 'is'. A thing 'is' when its essence is combined with its existence, and this entails a certain proportion or harmony which is constitutive of beauty. This means that everything is beautiful in so far as it 'is', because it 'is' in virtue of a concordance of essence with existence. Something is beautiful in so far as it 'is', and it 'is' in so far as it is beautiful; it possesses beauty in virtue of its proportion. Integrity in turn is a kind of proportion. Aquinas equates it with perfection, and perfection means the complete realization of whatever it is that the thing is supposed to be. As regards clarity, we know that for Aquinas it is connected with the notion of participation: all things participate in the divine clarity by virtue of their form. Particular things are therefore beautiful because of their form.[42] Clarity for Aquinas is therefore a property of form; it is an ontological property involving participation in life and being.

It thus becomes clear that Aquinas has uncovered a profound richness, previously undetected, in the constitutive elements of beauty (*proportio, integritas* and *claritas*) by placing them within the context of his metaphysical system. It is also beyond all doubt that beauty has a profound metaphysical worth for Aquinas, and the best way to uncover this worth is to examine it within the context of a metaphysical conceptual framework, something which he does. All Aquinas' statements concerning beauty or beautiful things must be therefore appraised in this metaphysical light: they cannot be viewed simply as statements of what Eco calls 'sociological fact', whatever that means.[43] They have a metaphysical

**40** ST, I, 5, 4 ad I.   **41** See Jan Aertsen, 'Beauty in the Middle Ages: a forgotten transcendental?' in *Medieval Philosophy and Theology* I (1991), 68–97, for a cogent exposition of this position. Chapter seven of our work offers a summary presentation of the position taken by Aertsen.   **42** See *Comm. Div. Nom.*, 4, 5.   **43** Eco, *Aesthetics*, p. 240, n. 22.

import. Maritain's statement that beauty is what gives pleasure on sight, *id quod visum placet*, cannot therefore be interpreted as a transformation of a statement of sociological fact into a metaphysical definition. It is simply a speculative development of a body of thought already imbued with a metaphysical worth.

Epistemological considerations support Maritain's interpretation. Clarity, as we know, is the capacity possessed by form to communicate itself through the medium of matter – this form which is the ontological foundation of beauty. This indicates that when a beautiful object's *claritas* is actualised by the aesthetic *visio* of a subject, the latter experiences its beauty. In simpler terms, it seems reasonable to argue that when we perceive a beautiful object, we *ipso facto* experience its beauty: there is no beautiful object that does not possess beauty along with its three constitutive elements.

A positive appraisal of Maritain's fidelity to the spirit of Aquinas' thought receives further support from Aquinas' definition of beauty: 'Beautiful refers to that which gives pleasure when it is perceived or contemplated' (*pulchrum autem dicatur id cujus ipsa apprehensio placet*).[44] The signification of the term *apprehensio* can be identified with the term *visio* in ST, 1, 5, 4 ad 1. If we substitute *visio* for *apprehensio* in the foregoing definition of the beautiful we get *pulchrum autem dicatur id cujus ipsa visio placet*. This is exactly the same as Maritain's definition of beauty as *id quod visum placet*. Maritain may be justly criticised for conflating different texts from Aquinas in formulating his own definition of beauty and for not alerting the reader to this fact; however, it does appear that the conflation itself is quite legitimate. Maritain's definition neither adds to nor detracts from Aquinas' own understanding of beauty.

We have now completed our consideration of the ontological constitution of beautiful objects under the aspects of *proportio, integritas,* and *claritas*, that is to say, we have considered the objective side of the aesthetic fact. It now time to turn to an examination of the subjective aspect, that is to say, those mental processes which lead to the experience of beauty on the part of the human subject.

---

**44** ST, 1–2, 27, 1 ad 3.

# CHAPTER THREE

# The foundations of the aesthetic *visio* in Aquinas' philosophy of mind

## Abstraction and the aesthetic visio *according to Eco*

S ENSORY COGNITION IS THE first step in the process whereby humans gain knowledge of reality. However, the knowledge afforded by sensation is incomplete; normally and naturally sensory activity terminates in the 'common sense' (*sensus communis*)[1] or what Klubertanz calls the 'first synthetic sense'.[2] Next an image known as a 'phantasm' is produced by the imagination, which is the locus of forms received from the senses, just as the receptive intellect is the locus of intellectual ideas.[3] However, Aquinas avers that phantasms, 'since they are likenesses of individuals and exist in corporeal organs, do not have the same mode of existence as the human intellect'.[4] This is because phantasms are imbued with materiality, whereas the intellect is of course immaterial. The intelligible content present in phantasms, therefore, is only potentially intelligible. In order that it may be rendered actually intelligible, the agent intellect[5] acts upon it and abstracts its intelligible species (*species impressa*). The agent intellect offers this *species impressa* to the possible intellect, which then produces a concept (*species expressa*).[6] It should be pointed out that this cognitive movement possesses absolutely no chronological structure, occurring as it does instantly and spontaneously; the distinctions of 'before' and 'after' pertain to the logical realm, not to the temporal. The movement cannot be divided into chronological steps, not even in the imagination: only the intellect can offer a logical analysis of

---

1 See *Comm. De Anima*, III, lect. 12 (773) and (774); see also ST, I, 1, 3 ad 2; I, 78, 4 ad 1, 2. 2 George P. Klubertanz, 'The internal senses in the process of cognition', *Modern Schoolman* 18 (1941) 28. 3 ST, I, 78, 4. 4 ST, I, 85, 1 ad 3. 5 See ST, I, 79, 3. 6 See ST, I, 85, I, 1 ad 3; also SCG, 4, 11, 6.

its structure. Immediately the eye perceives something, the act of abstraction occurs.[7]

Abstraction, which means the knowledge of an intelligible species, is a kind of knowledge that transcends individual circumstances and whatever accidents may be attached to the subject. It does not of course completely prescind from the matter with which the form is linked. Thus, for instance, the intellect 'cannot understand the snub-nosed without thinking of nose'.[8] In this sense, knowledge of the universal entails some reference to the matter in which the universal is particularised and concretised. Because matter is correlative to form, the knowledge of natural forms affords some knowledge of matter.[9] In one of his first works, *De Ente et Essentia*, Aquinas offers us a further insight into what is meant here. Here he introduces the notions of designated and undesignated matter. A thing is said to be designated (*designatum, signatum*) when it can be pointed out with the finger. This is true of an individual concrete thing, but not of an abstract nature or essence. The definition of the latter, however, includes undesignated matter. Thus in the definition of man, for instance, 'we do not put this particular bone and this particular flesh, but bone and flesh absolutely, which are the undesignated matter of man'.[10]

If the apprehension of beauty consisted simply in this awareness of matter's engagement with form, the act of *simplex apprehensio* would thus provide the conditions for an aesthetic judgment. However, the awareness of matter would be very slight. Aquinas refers to it as knowledge *aliquo modo* which, from *De Ente et Essentia*, seems to mean the knowledge of designated matter afforded by knowledge of undesignated matter. Certainly, the individual concrete object itself is not known in the act of abstraction. However, we can attain to knowledge of particulars by link-

---

7 'This simple and direct apprehension of reality by the intellect presupposes no conscious or original activity on its part. It is an operation of a mind that acts according to its nature and under the impetus of an external reality rather than the free activity of a mind that dominates and enriches reality': Étienne Gilson, *The philosophy of St Thomas Aquinas*, trans. Edward Bullough (New York, 1924), p. 272.  **8** *Comm. De Anima*, III, 8, 717.  **9** See *De Veritate*, 10, 4.  **10** *De Ente et Essentia*, 2, 4, trans. by Armand Maurer CSB, *On being and essence* (Toronto, 1968).

ing universal intellectual ideas with sensory experience. Aquinas posits
that the intellect can know the singular indirectly by turning back upon
the sense image (phantasm) from which it abstracts the species. The intellect therefore acquires some kind of knowledge of the singular on account
of its dynamic union with imagination.[11]

Eco posits that the kind of knowledge of the individual just delineated is markedly incomplete, and also fails to fulfill the requirements for
an aesthetic experience.[12] He argues that the contemplation of an object
as beautiful (*sub specie pulchri*) is the contemplation of a complex, formal
reality – a complex, formal reality which possesses a structural tension
among all its elements, especially in its metaphysical structure. Proportion
is not just a harmony among the sensible parts: this is one kind of proportion, admittedly, but one of the most elementary. The significance of
proportion is somewhat more profound than that (as should be evident
from our exposition of this notion in chapter two and from what we will
say later). As we saw, there are various kinds of proportion: the suitability of matter for the requirements of its *form*, the harmony between
essence and existence, the adequacy of a thing's function to what its nature
demands. Integrity consists in the conformity between what a thing actually is and what it ought to be according to the demands of its nature. We
judge the integrity of a thing by measuring it against its concept and
noting the degree of correspondence between what it is and what it ought
to be. In Eco's estimation, rational knowledge of the object is therefore a
necessary prerequisite for aesthetic appreciation of it.[13] This means that,
for Eco, the aesthetic *visio* cannot occur prior to the act of abstraction,
nor during that act, nor just after it. It occurs, rather, at the end of the
second operation of the intellect, that is to say, in the judgment.

In Eco's estimation, judgment is the only act which can provide the
kind of knowledge of a thing which is necessary in order to contemplate
it as beautiful, *sub specie pulchri*. He quotes the following passage from
Aquinas to support his position:

**11** See *De Veritate*, 2, 6; also *De Veritate*, 10, 5 and ST, 1, 86, 1.  **12** Eco, *Aesthetics*, p. 190.
**13** Ibid.

> The human intellect does not immediately, in first apprehending a thing, have complete knowledge; rather, it first apprehends only one aspect of the thing – namely, its whatness [*quidditas*], which is the primary and proper object of the intellect – and only then can it understand the properties, accidents and relationships incidental to the thing's essence. Accordingly, it must necessarily either combine one apprehension with another or separate them.[14]

It is clear that, in Eco's estimation, for an object to be appreciated as fully as possible in all its beauty by the aesthetic *visio*, its formal aspects must be discerned in their completeness. He posits that this discernment cannot be effected by means of the act by which the intellect conceives the quiddities of things. Rather, an act of joining and separating (*compositio* and *divisio*) on the part of the intellect is required. It is therefore to *compositio* and *divisio* that we now turn our attention.

## Compositio, divisio *and the aesthetic* visio

Aquinas, following Aristotle, distinguishes between two operations of the intellect: one by which it forms the simple quiddities of things (such as what man or animal is); the second by which it joins and divides concepts by affirmation or denial. Whereas the first of these operations does not involve truth or falsity, the second does, just as in the case of the proposition which is its sign.[15] Thus judgment, which pertains to the second operation of the intellect, is a purely synthetic act, as the term *compositio* suggests. Truth and falsity reside in the positing of this synthesis by affirmation or denial.

Lonergan offers an enlightening explanation, in terms of matter, form and existence, of Aquinas' understanding of judgment. Lonergan compares the terms of a judgment to matter and the synthesis of the terms to form; the act of positing a synthesis by means of affirmation or denial

**14** ST, I, 85, 5.  **15** *De Veritate*, 14, I.

he then likens to existence, which actuates the conjunction of matter and form.[16] It is precisely (in the case of composite substances) in the composition of matter and form, or also the combination of subject and accident, that the ground of the act of composition wrought by the intellect resides. This real composition in things serves as the foundation and cause of the truth in the combination produced by the intellect and expressed in words. Aquinas explains:

> For example, when I say, 'Socrates is a man,' the truth of this enunciation is caused by combining the form *humanity* with *the individual matter* by means of which Socrates is *this* man; and when I say, 'Man is white,' the cause of the truth of this enunciation is the combining of whiteness with the subject. It is similar in other cases. And the same thing is evident in the case of separation.[17]

It is clear that truth does not consist in a subjective mental synthesis. It is rather the correspondence of mental composition with real composition, or of mental division with real division. Falsity, on the other hand, is the noncorrespondence of mental composition with real division, or of mental division to real composition.[18]

In speaking of *compositio* we must avoid the mistake of thinking that two concepts merge into one. This can never happen; concepts always remain distinct. However, while two concepts may remain distinct as concepts, they may cease to constitute two separate intelligibilities and may merge into one. Thus 'commensurability and the diagonal are sometimes understood separately, making two distinct intelligible objects; but when combined they make one object which the mind understands all together'.[19] In composition there is a progression from two acts of understanding, expressed singly in two concepts, to one act of understanding, expressed in the combination of two concepts.

**16** Bernard Lonergan, *Verbum: word and idea in Aquinas*, ed. David. B. Burrell (London, 1967), p. 49. **17** *In Metaphys.*, 9, lect. 11 (1898). **18** Ibid., 1896; *In Metaphys.*, lect. 4 (1225). **19** *Comm. De Anima*, 3, lect. 11 (749).

In order to appreciate the ontological constitution of an object judgment is necessary, for by judgment alone is it possible to determine the adequacy of matter to its substantial form, of matter to its action, and so on. According to Eco, therefore, judgment is necessary if we are to contemplate an object *sub specie pulchri*.[20] He does allow that our senses may be stimulated by sensible proportion during the act of abstraction, and that we may experience an instinctive pleasure in it. Only the act of judgment, however, can enable us to determine whether a proportion is adequate to our capacity to experience it and to our psychological needs, and whether it also conforms, for instance, to the laws of musical composition. 'A quick and easy submission to the allure of harmony' can, according to Eco, produce a kind of pleasure that is 'aesthetic in embryo'.[21] However, genuine and complete aesthetic pleasure can ensue only when a person grasps the reasons for the harmony, the different ways in which it is realised, and all of its intricate workings. For Eco, therefore, judgment of one kind or another is a necessary prerequisite for aesthetic pleasure.

In viewing an aesthetic artifact, consciousness beholds a complex interplay of structures, multiple interrelations of forms which combine into increasingly inclusive forms. The intellect cannot fully comprehend this profound and complex order in a mere instant: it must join and separate, in a series of judgments which predicate of things their reality and categorial richness. Such understanding is only gradually attained. The intellect seeks to define the object, to plumb its depths and its meaning, its substantial and its accidental structure. It seeks to know the object in analytical detail and, at the end of the process, it will 'see' the object as true and desire it as good. Consequently, argues Eco, a disinterested perception concentrating upon formal values can occur only after the judgment has been made. Hence, aesthetic experience can take place at that point alone. There may, of course, be a desire for this kind of aesthetic *visio* during the quest for the judgment of truth, but it can be realised only following the act of judgment.[22]

---

**20** Eco, *Aesthetics*, p. 197.   **21** Ibid., 198.   **22** Ibid., 199.

On the basis of the understanding of the aesthetic *visio* just outlined, Eco rejects Maritain's contention that aesthetic pleasure is a total, complete kind of pleasure in that 'it is experienced prior to the labor of abstraction'.[23] On the contrary, he maintains that it is total and complete in that it arises precisely from the cessation of the efforts of abstraction and judgment. Aesthetic pleasure, according to Eco, follows upon a *cessation* of effort, not its absence. It is a sense of exaltation in a form which has been discerned and loved with a disinterested love, the kind of love which is possible in regard to a formal structure.[24] Given our understanding of Aquinas' doctrine concerning the second operation of the intellect, we must agree with Eco on this issue, although we will later argue that there are resources in Aquinas' thought which can take beyond mere considerations of form when dealing with experience of aesthetic objects. It is very difficult to see how Maritain's position can be reconciled with the Thomistic epistemological principles which we have delineated. Put simply, while these principles demand an act of abstraction as a prerequisite for the aesthetic *visio*, Maritain argues for an experience of the beautiful which is prior to and which indeed does not involve abstraction.

## *Visio in actu est claritas in actu*

In chapter two, we saw that 'clarity' is the communicative capacity which form possesses, but which is only actualised by someone's 'looking at', or 'seeing', the object. In other words, the actualisation of an object's property of clarity is identical with the actualisation of a capacity for 'seeing' or 'looking'. In order to express this reality, we coined the formula *visio in actu est claritas in actu*. It is now our task to draw out some of the implications of this assertion. As a preliminary remark, we may say that it implies that, only to the extent that a subject actualises his aesthetic *visio* in relation to an aesthetic artifact by means of a series of judgments pertaining to the second operation of the intellect, will he be able to encounter and experience the artifact's aesthetic quality.

23 Ibid., 200.  24 Ibid.

---

Such an attitude runs counter to the opinion that any kind of intellectual analysis is destructive of true aesthetic experience. Aesthetic experience, according to this line of thinking, simply consists in soaking up the experience which the aesthetic artifact offers and ignoring any and all intellectual considerations. Anyone is held to be capable of such an experience, provided he is open enough to it. To adopt such a stance is to discount the sincere claim of many people that their experience of artistic artifacts in a particular medium has been enriched, and continues to be enriched, by means of intellectual endeavor. It is our contention that no aesthetic theory based on the thought of Aquinas can countenance such a stance, which we may designate anti-intellectualist.

Another attitude often encountered insists that all aesthetic judgments are subjective. Thus, if one person believes, for example, that painting A is better than painting B, while another person is of the opinion that painting B is the better of the two, neither person can in principle be right or wrong. Some argue that this point of view is practically self-evident from the fact that people regularly disagree regarding matters of aesthetic judgment. Such a position, of course, denies all possibility of objectivity in aesthetic judgments.[25]

According to the formula *visio in actu est claritas in actu*, aesthetic experience at its height is a fusion of both the objective and the subjective poles of the human experience of reality. Just as the sense faculty which is actualised is the same as the sense-object which is actualised

---

**25** Interestingly enough and somewhat surprisingly, Gilson adopts this stance. He asserts: 'Esthetic judgments are both dogmatic and unjustifiable. Every one of us may check the accuracy of this fact by observing himself; besides, the shortest conversation with other art lovers will show them to be what we ourselves are, positive in their statements, even inclined to exaggerate and defend them forcefully when they are challenged. But they remain, if not incapable of arguing in favor of their opinion, at least powerless to bring any convincing objective justification of it': *The arts of the beautiful*, p. 40. Although he defines the beautiful as 'the good of an intelligent sensibility', Gilson does in our estimation overemphasise the sensible aspect of aesthetic experience to the total neglect of the intellectual aspect. George Steiner is another who adopts this kind of position. Commenting upon adverse criticism directed at great artists, he says: 'The instruments of articulation, the sinews of syntactic and of semantic coherence, the reach of persuasive intelligibility in these 'inadmissible' propositions are of exactly the same status as in their antitheses': *Real presences* (London, 1989), p. 62.

(*sensus in actu est sensibile in actu*), and the actualisation of an object of thought is the same as the actualisation of the capacity for thinking (*intellectus in actu est intellectum in actu*), so too the actualisation of the human subject's capacity for aesthetic *visio* is the same as the actualisation of an object's clarity (*visio in actu est claritas in actu*). However, it can often happen that the individual subject fails to actualise his aesthetic *visio* in such a way that the subjective and objective poles of the experience are completely merged in one another. It might indeed be argued that the union of the subjective and objective poles of aesthetic experience, which gives rise to an experience in which distinctions of subject and object are completely overcome, is something that simply never comes to pass in reality. It is purely an ideal, something to which we can all aspire but which we can never reach. Different people actualise their capacity for aesthetic experience to varying degrees, some more, some less. To the extent that they do this, the aesthetic artifact will offer itself to them for contemplation, for its ontological constitution is such that it is always ready to be judged by a human subject. The more the subjectivity of the aesthetic *visio* is actualised, the more the capacity of the artifact to communicate its objective constitution, that is to say, its clarity, is actualised.

As will we come to see, however, human subjectivity is always conditioned subjectivity, that is to say, it can never exist in a vacuum but is informed by a complex array of historical, cultural, social, political, and familial factors, to name but a few. Given this reality, experience of beauty is rendered somewhat more complex – but also much richer – than it otherwise would be, that is to say, than it would be if an account of the life of mind divorced from affectivity were true to the nature of things. It is of course not true to the nature of things, and such an account is demonstrably not that of Aquinas – at least not when the latter is expounded in the context of his overall understanding of the human being, as we shall see. Our own interpretation of Aquinas on the life of mind will provide some explanation of what is a commonplace in aesthetic judgements, namely a certain lack of agreement.

## The inseparability of receptivity and activity in human operations

We have seen that, according to the formula, *visio in actu est claritas in actu*, there is in aesthetic experience a fusion, at least to some degree, of both subjective and objective poles. The reasonableness of this interpretation receives support from Pareyson in his discussion of interpretation and contemplation, the term of the interpretative process.[26] The whole discussion therefore revolves around the role of the subject in aesthetic experience. For Pareyson, it is clear that there is no such thing as pure subjectivity in the process of interpretation. It goes without saying that an interpretation is always the interpretation of an individual subject, the activity proper to the person who interprets, an attempt on the part of the subject to penetrate the meaning of the object. On the other hand, we must emphasise at the same time the role of the object in interpretation, for interpretation is always an interpretation of something: it is an activity which engages a definite object. Interpretation cannot exist without an object.

Interpretation in fact implies the reciprocity of receptivity and activity. Receptivity and activity are mutually implicative in the interpretative process. On the one hand, the object resonates in the subject, that is to say, receptivity becomes activity. This is evident from the fact that, on receiving an object, subjectivity begins to work on it. On the other hand, there is a certain agreement with the object, that is, an activity which disposes itself to receive. On the one hand, on beholding the object the subject is stimulated to develop his grasp of its meaning, and this development is proper to the subject alone, being due exclusively to his activity. On the other hand, his efforts to sharpen and refine his vision render his receptivity deliberate and open, submitting it in obedience to the object in an exercise of fidelity. For Pareyson, 'receptivity is refined by means of activity and activity aims at receptivity'.[27] He opines that they are in fact inter-

26 Luigi Pareyson, *Estetica: teoria della formatività* (Bologna, 1960), pp 151–88.  27 Pareyson, *Estetica*, p. 155.

twined, one with the other, feeding one another, sustaining one another, referring to one another and implying one another.

The foregoing account of interpretation is based on the premise that in all human operations receptivity and activity are inseparably linked: receptivity implies the presence of some activity, and, conversely, activity implies the presence of some receptivity. Any human function is both receptive and active, and not one or the other in an exclusive manner – because receptivity without activity would issue in pure passivity, while activity not arising from some initial receptivity would more correctly be termed creativity. Receptivity and activity in human operations are indistinguishable because they constitute one another.

Pareyson's comments on the reciprocity of receptivity and activity in the interpretative process provide support, from a distinguished author belonging to a very different philosophical tradition from the Thomistic one, for our own contention that aesthetic experience implies and demands some degree of union between subjectivity and objectivity. A beautiful thing possesses an objective structure such that it offers itself to contemplation. In response to this stimulus, the intellect, by means of a series of judgments, seeks to penetrate the meaning of the object. At the term of this series of judgments, the intellect rests and the will delights in the apprehension attained. In so far as the intellect penetrates the meaning of the object it is conformed to this meaning, and to this extent the subjective apprehension of the intellect is rendered objective. It is in this 'objectivisation' of subjectivity that the will delights. Thus we can say that aesthetic experience is constituted by the delight which results from the objectivisation of subjectivity.

The term of a series of judgments which result in the delight of the will in the apprehension of the intellect provides a new starting point for further intellectual inquiry aiming at a more profound appreciation of the object of inquiry. The intellect naturally seeks its own good, namely truth, and by means of another set of judgments corrects its previous understanding of the object, increases its grasp and deepens its apprehension. This further actualisation of the intellect entails as a necessary corollary a further actualisation of the intelligibility of the object. The further actualisation of both intellect and object results in an increased actualisation of both the subject's aesthetic *visio* and the object's *claritas*. The will delights in the new apprehension reached by the intellect, an apprehension which has penetrated more deeply into the intelligibility of the object than the previous apprehension managed to do. Subjectivity has been further 'objectivised' in the further actualisation of the intellect: the intellect is more conformed with its object, and in the aesthetic *visio* the subject experiences a more profound union with the object.

The foregoing can be repeated time after time. The dynamic process that issues in aesthetic *visio* can thus be understood as a kind of dialectic. The subject's intellectual grasp and consequent aesthetic experience of an object is ever susceptible to further development. It can never be claimed that an individual has developed his capacity for aesthetic appreciation to such an extent that he is not capable of an ever-deeper appreciation. And the deeper his appreciation, the more his aesthetic *visio* is actualised, the more his subjectivity becomes one with objectivity, that is, the more it is objectivised. Ever-deepening aesthetic experience of an object is an experience of ever-deepening union with that object.

The pleasure of aesthetic experience, however, can come about only when the reasons for the harmony, the different ways in which it is realised, and its complex inner workings are apprehended. The judgments by which such apprehension is effected provide the basis, moreover, for comparing the relative artistic merits of artistic artifacts belonging to the same medium, for they make manifest in the first place the extent to which each artifact conforms to the laws operative in the relevant medium. Further judgment by the intellect can then yield a comparison between two or more artistic artifacts and this judgment (it can reasonably be argued on the basis of what we have said), possesses a certain objective character.[28] Indeed, the greater the extent to which intellectual

---

28 This position, although it may not be the most popular these days, is embraced by Mary Mothersill. She writes: 'Although the judgment of taste is categorical, items may be ranked in order of beauty, and an aesthetic theory ought to provide some account of judgments of the form "x is more beautiful than y"': *Beauty restored* (Oxford, 1984), p. 378.

appreciation of the artifact is actualised, the more the aesthetic *visio* is actualised; and the more the aesthetic *visio* is actualised, the more in turn it becomes one with the artifact offering itself for contemplation. In other words, subjectivity and objectivity become more and more identified according as the aesthetic *visio* is actualised by the actualisation of the intellectual appreciation of the artifact. We might say that the subjectivity of the aesthetic *visio* is objectivised. On the other hand, however, it is also true that the objectivity of the artistic artifact is also subjectivised by the aesthetic *visio*.

At this point in our discussion we cannot develop this important aspect of aesthetic experience. We will, nevertheless, take it up in chapter six when we draw out the implications for aesthetic experience of a theory of judgment *per modum inclinationis*. It suffices here to note that any aesthetic theory based on Thomistic principles will necessarily avoid the two extremes of subjectivism and objectivism. Our contention is that the more authentic the aesthetic experience of an individual is, the more it will transcend any such distinction.

## *The* intellectus-ratio *distinction and the aesthetic* visio

In order both to clarify and to support our understanding of the aesthetic *visio* as outlined in the preceding section, let us briefly examine the distinction Aquinas draws between *intellectus* and *ratio*.[29] In *De Veritate* 15, 1, Aquinas explains the difference between these two notions in terms of movement and rest, generation and existence. The principle and terminus of the movement of reason is understanding:

> It [reason] is related to understanding as to its source and term. It is related to it as its source because the human mind could not

**29** See Colm McClements, 'The distinction *intellectus-ratio* in the philosophy of Thomas Aquinas: a historical and critical study' (PhD diss., Université Catholique de Louvain, 1990), for an extended treatment of this distinction.

move from one thing to another unless the movement started from some simple perception of the truth, and this perception is understanding of principles. Similarly, the movement of reason would not reach anything certain unless there were an examination of that which it came upon through the discursive movement of the mind. This examination proceeds to first principles, the point to which reason pursues its analysis. As a result, we find that understanding is the source of reasoning in the process of discovery and its term in that of judging.

Human reasoning has its basis in the specifically human mode of understanding. Animals cannot understand, and therefore do not reason. Separated substances, on the other hand, see the truth of things in a single intuition; they do not know discursively by way of reason, but rather see immediately by means of understanding (*intellectus*).

Man enjoys a special position in created reality in that 'he is, as it were, the horizon and boundary of spiritual and corporeal nature; he is, as it were, the medium between both'.[30] This mode of being entails a special mode of knowing. The human is the lowest-ranking spiritual being; as a result man participates in intellectuality only in an imperfect manner. Just as in the material world primary matter is in potency to sensible forms, so too the human intellect is in potency to intelligible objects. As Aertsen explains, 'man possesses a transcendental openness, but he must still appropriate reality by actual knowing'.[31]

Rationality has its origin in this potentiality or imperfection of the human soul; it is founded in the fact that the human being is an incarnate mind, and hence dependent upon sense experience. The movement of reason therefore proceeds 'from what is sensible to what is intelligible'.[32] Since sense knowledge is concerned with the particular, reason is forced to engage with multiplicity in order to attain to the one, simple

30 *In III Sent.*, prol. See SCG, 2, 68 [6]. A discussion of this theme is found in G. Verbeke, 'Man as a "frontier"', in *Aquinas and problems of his time*, ed. G. Verbeke and D. Verhelst (Leuven, 1976), pp 195–223.  31 Jan Aertsen, *Nature and creature: Thomas Aquinas's way of thought* (New York, 1988), p. 193.  32 *In II Sent.*, d. 3, q. 1, a. 6, sol.

truth.[33] Human nature must employ reason in order to come to knowledge of the truth.

Human knowing, therefore, proceeds by way of reason (*per viam rationis*), where *ratio* is understood as a mode of knowing distinct from *intellectus*. *Intellectus* is elucidated etymologically by Aquinas as *intus-legere*: 'And one is said to understand (*intelligere*) because in some sense he reads (*legit*) the truth within (*intus*) the very essence of the thing.'[34] Pure spiritual beings enjoy this kind of knowledge. They know the truth of things in a single intuition, not discursively. The spiritual substances do not have to acquire truth by consideration of a multiplicity and diversity of sensible things. Rather, the kind of knowledge they enjoy is simple and uniform; their understanding is godlike (*deiformis*).[35]

As already stated, the origin and end of the movement of reason is *intellectus*. The origin is *intellectus* because discursiveness must begin from insights which are not acquired through reasoning but which are apprehended immediately. The terminus is *intellectus*, because when reason has reduced multiplicity to unity it no longer reasons but understands.

It is important to point out that it is by the same power that we understand and reason. In other words, the acts of reason and of intellect are not the acts of distinct powers. 'Reason itself is called understanding because it shares in the intellectual simplicity, by reason of which it begins and through which it terminates its proper activity.'[36] The relation of reason to intellect is explained by the analogy of movement to rest. Just as each natural movement proceeds from something which is at rest and ends in something at rest, so too human reasoning has intellect as its starting point and terminus. The movement of reason there-

---

**33** 'Reason differs from intellect as multitude does from unity ... It is proper to reason to be dispersed in consideration of many things and to gather together one simple cognition from them. Whence Dionysius says in the *De Divinis Nominibus* (c. 7) that souls are rational in as much as they consider the truth of existing things in a diffuse manner': *In Boeth. De trin.* 6, 1 ad tertiam quaestionem. **34** *De Veritate* 15, 1. **35** 'By virtue of the fact that an angel has a godlike understanding, it considers things without movement. In this way an angel is said to differ from a soul, because the soul does not know by means of godlike understanding but by way of rational inquiry': *In II Sent.*, d. 3, q. 1, a. 6. See also *SCG*, 3, 91. **36** *De Veritate* 15, 1.

fore has a circular structure: it begins from the one and simple, and proceeds by the way of multiplicity in order to terminate once again in the
one. 'The procession of reason is a certain turning around like a circle'.[37]

As pointed out by Colm McClements, *intellectus* is not an absolute
end at which *ratio* terminates: 'For reason is to be understood as a con-
tinuous movement which is punctuated by a series of intellectual
insights.'[38] This implies that the movement of reason is dialectical. Indeed,
many commentators have spoken of Aquinas' understanding of reason
in these terms.[39] McClements draws our attention to the fact that 'reason
is for ever discovering and resolving, and from what is resolved, is for
ever discovering more. From properly universal causes, the result of a
prior resolution and grasped according to an intellectual insight, reason
moves on towards new discovery.'[40]

The dynamism inherent in the movement of reason, which we have
just briefly delineated, is clearly operative in the unfolding and development of the aesthetic *visio*. In studying a particular artifact, I posit a series
of judgments. At the term of these judgments, I rest in the delight
afforded to me by the understanding attained. No longer does *ratio* proceed by way of multiplicity; rather, it terminates in unity, which is grasped
by *intellectus*. On the basis of this resolution – itself the result of a prior
resolution and grasped by an act of intellectual insight – reason can move
on towards new discovery, that is to say, towards a deeper aesthetic appreciation of the object in question. This movement of reason once more
terminates in understanding. In this way, aesthetic contemplation can
be regarded as the origin and term of each act of rational enquiry, these
acts endeavoring to penetrate the artistic artifact ever more deeply.

Eldridge offers concrete illustrations of how the movement of reason,
terminating in an enriched understanding, can lead to a deeper aesthetic
appreciation of a particular artistic artifact, although he does not express
himself in these terms. Various avenues of rational enquiry can inform

---

**37** *Comm. Div. Nom.* 7, lectio 2, 713. **38** 'The distinction *intellectus-ratio* in the philosophy of Thomas Aquinas', p. 310. **39** McClements, however, opines that 'the reconstruction of such a teaching in Thomas would seem to be somewhat difficult even if one
must consider that Thomas did conceive reason in this sense': ibid. **40** Ibid., 311.

one's appreciation of a work of art – 'Spirit-of-the-Age, biographical, sociopolitical-structural, editorial-physical, or artistic-improvisatory'. Thus, for example, the works of Shakespeare or Wordsworth or Austen can have different meanings for someone after he has read and taken to heart Freud or Marx, or after having read Eliot or Larkin. In a similar way, Schubert can 'sound different affectively and expressively after hearing minimalist music or Wagner or after reading Adorno or McClary or Dalhaus'.[41]

When we avail of different approaches to appraising the significance of a work of art, our understanding of it becomes more comprehensive. Because we generally have shared understandings of what constitutes a work of art, to change from one structure of understanding it to another is not, in the words of Stanley Fish, 'a rupture but a modification of the interests and concerns that are already in place'. Because, moreover, they are already in place, 'they constrain the direction of their own modification'. Fish continues: 'The [hearer, viewer, reader] is already in a situation informed by tacitly known purposes and goals, and [after encountering a new reading] ends up in another situation whose purposes and goals stand in some elaborated relation (of contrast, opposition, expansion, extension) to those they supplant.'[42]

## Visio in actu est claritas in actu: *educational implications*

To complete our treatment of the aesthetic *visio*, we would like to point out very briefly that the formula *visio in actu est claritas in actu* is not bereft of educational implications. (This we do, cognisant of the fact that an adequate treatment of the subject would merit a full-scale study.) We make this claim on the basis that the actualisation of the aesthetic *visio* entails, *ipso facto*, the actualisation of the cognitive and appetitive rational powers of intellect and will. Rationality is peculiar to and constitutive of

---

**41** Richard Eldridge, *An introduction to the philosophy of art* (Cambridge, 2003), p. 147.
**42** Stanley Fish, 'Is there a text in this class?', in S. Fish, *Is there a text in this class* (Cambridge, MA, 1980), pp 530B–531A, quoted in Eldridge, *Introduction*, p. 148.

human being; it can be regarded as the specifying potentiality of the human species. Now a thing's being is perfected when and to the extent that it performs instances of its specific operation, actualising its specifying potentiality: 'Anything whatever is perfect to the extent to which it is in actuality, since potentiality without actuality is imperfect.'[43] Thus in the basic, metaphysical sense of 'perfect', a thing is perfect in its kind to the extent that it actualises the specifying potentiality of its form.

The aesthetic *visio*, as we have described it, engages the human specifying potentialities of intellect and will in their entirety, for beautiful things are those which, when seen, give pleasure.[44] While it may be said of all specifically human activity that both intellect and will are involved therein on account of the unitary composite nature of the human person, we must add certain qualifications in order to be true to the reality. Thus, at one extreme, the kind of rational enquiry proper to mathematics is indeed informed by the operation of the will – for truth is the good of the intellect, and the will delights when the intellect attains to its good; the action of the will in this case however is not anywhere nearly as prominent as that of the intellect. It is as if most of the person's spiritual energy were directed to the intellect and its operation. At the other extreme we can take the example of a person, lacking any intellectual formation whatsoever in ethics, who is faced with a moral situation demanding immediate action. While the operation of the intellect is certainly present in this case, it is the will that engages most of the person's spiritual energy. In the case of the aesthetic *visio*, in contrast to these two extremes, both intellect and will are prominently engaged: the will delights in the fruits of intellectual endeavor. The operation of neither recedes, as it were, into the background.

Aesthetic experience, therefore, is something specifically human, involving the actualisation of potentialities specifying human being. Now, considered *absolutely* (*simpliciter*), every being is an instantiation of a certain substantial form. In other words it is the existence of a thing of a certain kind, and this existence admits of neither more nor less. This gen-

---

**43** ST, 1–2, 3, 2.  **44** ST, 1, 5, 4 ad 1.

eral truth applies to human beings as much as to anything else. In this absolute sense, a person can be neither more nor less a human being than anyone else. However, when the specifying potentiality of a thing is actualised it can be said, *relatively speaking* (*secundum quid*), to be a better specimen of the kind of thing it is supposed to be. Thus, a human person who actualises his cognitional and volitional potentialities becomes a better specimen of human being. Everyday language reflects this, as when we say of someone that he is a better person as result of some experience or other.

The subject of aesthetic experience is consequently rendered a better person, *relatively speaking*. Human being can be said to be more perfect the more it conforms to the rational mode of being proper to it; that is to say, the more it realises its proper form, the more perfect it becomes. And, of course, the more perfectly something realises its form the more beautiful it becomes. Thus, a person engaged in the manner of rational enquiry necessary for the realisation of aesthetic *visio*, or who is delighting in the fruits of that enquiry, can be said to have become a more beautiful person. Not only is true aesthetic experience an experience of beauty, it is immediately productive of beauty. Moreover, it is productive of beauty in the only creature capable of producing works of beauty. We can therefore describe artistic creativity as a means whereby man can humanise his fellow human beings or be humanised by them. When the beautiful is divorced from the aesthetic, however, art can also become a means of dehumanisation.

Since education is a means which facilitates the process of human becoming, or the development of human beings *qua* human beings, the relevance of the foregoing becomes clearly manifest. In a technological world where utilitarian considerations reign supreme, it is no great secret that the fine arts are accorded a very minor place in the curricula of many education systems. If what we have claimed is true, however, then surely the arts ought to be accorded a more important role. In this regard, we are thinking in particular of imparting skills to *all* students relative to the appreciation of beauty in its various manifestations, particularly in the fine arts. We emphasise 'to *all* students', because it can often happen that only those who have a creative flair in a particular artistic medium are in fact encouraged in that direction. This means that those who have no creative ability in any particular medium are not given the opportunity to actualise themselves in this way as human beings. They are condemned to a relatively impoverished human existence, a life lacking in the appreciation of beauty, and in the concomitant beauty actualised in the human person as a result of this kind of experience. Their lives are less beautiful than they could and indeed should be. An educational system which relegates the arts to a secondary status stands condemned for limiting those entrusted to its care to a more mundane existence than might otherwise be the case, as well as for failing to actualise their humanity to the greatest extent possible.

We argue that there is a strong case for introducing students to the formal analysis of artistic artifacts and to an understanding of their place within a wider aesthetic context. This we do on the basis of our understanding of the dynamic operative in the aesthetic act, which we have encapsulated in the formula *visio in actu est claritas in actu*. This approach, when adopted with due honesty by student and teacher alike, should enable the student to penetrate the meaning of artifacts to some extent, thereby conforming his intellect to their meaning. This conforming of intellect to meaning will render the student's subjective apprehension more objective. In other words, on the basis of what we have said concerning the inseparability of receptivity and activity in human operations, education in the arts would facilitate an objectivisation of subjectivity. Subjectivity would then be trained and habituated to delight in higher forms of beauty, and not to mistake that which approaches the domain of sensuality for true beauty. Moreover, as will become clear later on, on account of the intrinsic connection between beauty, on the one hand, and truth and goodness, on the other – for beauty is in fact a function of truth and goodness, it is the good perceived as true – formation of students in appreciation of truly beautiful artworks can facilitate their moral and religious formation.

# CHAPTER FOUR

# Maritain's theory of art:
# epistemological foundations

A T THIS POINT IN our study we have completed our exegesis and development of Aquinas' embryonic aesthetic theory following the lead of what is generally considered to be the most definitive exposition to date, namely that of Umberto Eco, an exposition which although accurate in so far as it goes is nonetheless defective in that it fails to consider Aquinas' understanding of rationality in its entirety. While it is true that Eco does make reference to the senses and the emotions in his exegesis of Aquinas' embryonic aesthetic theory, he nevertheless disregards the latter's radically unitary conception of human being. He consequently ignores the influence of sense and emotion on the life of reason, that is to say, he is seemingly unaware that, for Aquinas, pure reason does not exist. In this respect Eco's interpretation of Aquinas on the life of reason follows in the tracks of those forms of post-Enlightenment Thomism which have sought to engage Aquinas with modernity, but which have unwittingly done so on modernity's own terms. Since reason is crucially central to the aesthetic fact for Aquinas, it is imperative that one's account of it be faithful to his overall teaching on this subject. Otherwise any purported theory of aesthetic perception according to the mind of Aquinas will be anything but that. Most likely it will be some kind of theory of aesthetic perception based on the principles found in the work of Aquinas and as viewed through the lens of Enlightenment rationalism.

Before offering a more adequate account of Aquinas' conception of the life of reason, let us first of all consider Maritain's theory of art, for central to this theory is the notion of knowledge through connaturality which he encountered in his intellectual mentor. While Maritain's theory of artistic creativity is not unproblematic with regard to its fidelity to Aquinas' thought, it nonetheless attempts to give an account of the role of sensibility and emotion in this experience. In this respect it moves beyond the sterile rationalism which increasingly came to plague the Thomist tradition up to quite recently. It therefore provides a contrast with Eco's approach to aesthetic perception and gives us a pointer as to how we might proceed in formulating a theory of aesthetic perception which will be faithful to Aquinas and which can also engage forcefully with contemporary debate concerning art and beauty.

## *Maritain and the notion of poetry in* Creative Intuition in Art and Poetry

Eco believes that the influence of Henri Bergson is ever at hand in Maritain's formulation of a theory of artistic production, particularly in his elaboration of the notion of poetic knowledge as a form of knowledge *through connaturality*. This notion, Eco argues, can be traced back to its source in Maritain's understanding of the aesthetic *visio*. Eco insists that Maritain, in his theory of artistic creativity, continues to display the same lack of historiographical concern which Eco believes is evident in *Art and Scholasticism*. Unlike his approach in *Art and Scholasticism*, however, Maritain does not pretend to be anything other than overtly speculative in developing his theory of artistic creativity. The manner of intuitionism which Maritain espouses, according to Eco, is something which 'the medieval philosopher, far from refuting, would not have understood'.[1]

Maritain's understanding of poetry receives its most developed treatment in *Creative Intuition in Art and Poetry*, written in an Anglo-Saxon ambience. This work is the result of deep reflection on contemporary art, and it is even more speculative in approach than his previous writings on aesthetic theory. By poetry Maritain means 'that intercommunication between the inner being of things and the inner being of the human Self which is a kind of divination'.[2] It obliges us 'to consider the intellect both in its secret wellsprings inside the human soul and as func-

1 *La definizione dell'arte* (Milan, 1968), p. 106.  2 *Creative intuition in art and poetry* (New York, 1953), p. 3.

tioning in a nonrational ... or nonlogical way'.[3] Further on in this chapter Maritain concludes that the poetic perception which animates art involves at the same time a disclosure and a manifestation, unintentional as it may be, of the human Self.[4] Consequently, he suggests that what grounds the creative act is an intellectual process unique to it alone and through which 'the Things and the Self are grasped together by means of a kind of experience or knowledge which has no conceptual expression and is expressed only in the artist's work'.[5]

This is *poetic knowledge*, and Maritain integrates it with the medieval conception of *recta ratio factibilium*. Thus even if art is a virtue of the practical intellect, the rules according to which the intellect operates are not in this case rigid canonical rules which precede the work. Rather, creative intuition is superimposed on these rules of making and animates them by means of an act which proceeds from the depths of the spirit.


## Poetic intuition


Maritain, having argued for the existence of a spiritual unconscious, posits that it is here that creative or artistic intuition can be thought to have its source. He thinks that there is in the spiritual unconscious of the intellect, in addition to the process which engenders concepts, a preconceptual or nonconceptual form of knowledge. It is precisely this nonconceptual form of knowledge, the essence of which is constituted by the subjectivity of the artist, which artistic creativity presupposes. Artistic creativity demands that the artist grasp his own subjectivity in order to create.

Unlike God, man does not know himself in the light of his own essence; he knows himself only by virtue of his knowledge of external things. Consequently he must deepen his knowledge of external reality, if he is to grow in self-knowledge. In like manner, it is only on condition that reality resound in him and that, in him, knowledge of both reality and of himself simultaneously awaken, that the artist may come

3 Ibid.   4 Ibid., p. 33.   5 Ibid., pp 33–4.

---

to know himself. In other words, poetry[6] involves 'the obscure knowing, by the poet, of his own subjectivity' along with 'the grasping, by the poet, of the objective reality of the outer and inner world' and this occurs 'not by means of concepts and conceptual knowledge, but by means of an obscure knowledge … through affective union'.[7] Consequently, artistic knowledge is not knowledge in the sense outlined by Maritain when speaking of the way in which concepts are formed. Rather, it is a manner of knowing in which the artist receives 'the objective reality of the outer and inner world' in the obscure recesses of his being. All that he perceives in external reality, he perceives not according to the law of speculative knowledge as something other than himself, but rather as inseparable from himself and from his own affectivity; it is something that is one with his being.

For Maritain, therefore, creative intuition is the artist's obscure grasping of his own self and of some aspect or relation of an external reality in a *knowledge through union, inclination,* or *connaturality* which is born in the spiritual preconscious and which comes to fruition in an artistic artifact. It now behoves us briefly to elucidate Maritain's understanding of *knowledge through connaturality* – a concept borrowed from Aquinas – as he applies it to artistic creativity.

## Artistic creativity and knowledge through connaturality

Maritain believes poetic or artistic knowledge to be a specific form of knowledge through union, inclination, or connaturality. Knowledge through connaturality refers to a basic distinction made by Aquinas when he explains that there are two different ways in which we can judge things pertaining to moral virtue. On the one hand, there is an intellectual knowledge of virtues, the kind of knowledge possessed by one who has studied moral science. A scientific moralist, by rational application of the principles of moral science, may form a correct judgment on moral

**6** 'Poetry' can understood here to mean any form of artistic creativity.  **7** *Creative intuition,* pp 114–15.

matters. Indeed, such a person may possibly know everything about virtue and yet not be virtuous.

On the other hand, we can possess a particular virtue in our powers of will and desire. In this sense we may be said to be in accordance with it or 'connatured' with it in our very being. When faced with a question about a virtue, say fortitude, a virtuous person consults the inner inclinations of his own being; he knows the right answer not through science, but through inclination. A virtuous person may possibly lack all knowledge of moral philosophy, but nonetheless know everything concerning the virtues – or at least everything a particular virtue requires in a particular situation – through being 'connatured' with them.

Knowledge through connaturality is not therefore rational knowledge. It is not knowledge acquired by means of the conceptual, logical and discursive exercise of reason. Here, the intellect operates together with the affective inclinations and dispositions of the will and is guided and shaped by them. However, knowledge through connaturality is a genuine form of knowledge, 'though obscure and perhaps incapable of giving account of itself'.[8]

For Maritain, poetic knowledge is a specific form of knowledge through inclination or connaturality; it is a knowledge through affective connaturality which pertains essentially to the creativity of the spirit and which expresses itself in a work of art. In this kind of knowledge, the artistic artifact (the poem, the painting, the musical composition) takes the place occupied in speculative knowledge by concepts and judgments. Poetic knowledge is inseparable from the productivity of the human spirit and, unable to issue in an internal concept, it issues instead in an external work. Poetic knowledge is fully expressed only when it issues in a work. Although it arises in a preconscious manner, it emerges into consciousness 'through an impact both emotional and intellectual'.[9]

Knowledge through connaturality as it pertains to poetic knowledge is effected by means of emotion. Thus, whereas concepts are the medium of science (or of scientific insight), emotion is the medium of poetic

**8** Ibid., p. 117. **9** Ibid., p. 118.

insight. However, it is not merely emotional because although it is effected through the instrumentality of feeling, it issues from the intellect. Creative knowledge is not something merely emotional or sentimental, because it is the intellect, not emotion, that knows.

As regards emotion itself, it is not the matter or material of the work to be made; a work of art does not express or depict the artist's emotion. Rather the emotion, which is the proper medium of creative intuition, gives form to a work of art as well as being the intentional[10] vehicle of reality known through inclination or connaturality. It is distinct from the merely subjective emotions and feelings of the artist considered as a human being. Although distinct from them, however, creative intuition lives from subjective emotions and feelings, while necessarily transmuting them.

The question which Maritain faces is how emotion can become an instrumental vehicle, analogous to the concept in speculative knowledge through which reality is grasped by the intellect. He argues that as in the case of other spheres where we encounter knowledge through connaturality, the soul 'suffers' things more than it learns them; it 'experiences them through resonance in subjectivity'.[11] Employing the notion which John of St Thomas developed in relation to mystical knowledge – *affectus transit in conditionem objecti* –[12] Maritain argues that emotion in artistic knowledge conveys into the depths of the artist's subjectivity, that is to say, into the spiritual unconscious of the intellect, in an analogical manner, the reality which the soul suffers. On the one hand, it permeates the entire soul, it saturates its very being, and thus 'certain particular aspects in things become connatural to the soul affected in this way'.[13] On the other hand, emotion is received into the vital inner recesses of intelligence. It is permeated by the light of the Illuminating Intellect and enters into dynamic contact with the soul's store of experience and

10 By the word 'intentional', Maritain understands the purely immaterial or suprasubjective tendential existence through which a thing – the object known, for example – is present in an 'instrument'. Thus a concept, since it is an instrument by means of which we know some particular reality, is an *intentio* towards its object. 11 *Creative intuition*, p. 122. 12 Joannis A.S. Thoma, *Cursus Theologicus*, vol. 6, *De Donis Spiritus Sancti*, d. 18, a. 4, n. 11 (Paris, 1885). 13 *Creative intuition*, p. 122.

memory. Emotion, thanks to the light of the Illuminating Intellect which now saturates it, is transformed into an instrument of intelligence judging through inclination or connaturality. Thus, emotion in this process of knowledge through connaturality between subjectivity and reality determines intelligence in its preconscious activity in a nonconceptual fashion. It conveys things other than itself in an intentional manner (that is to say, in a state of immateriality), and thus possesses an objective status analogous to that of the concept. It becomes for the intellect a means whereby the things, along with the deeper, invisible realities contained in them or connected with them are understood and known obscurely. Hence, poetic or creative intuition, according to Maritain, is engendered in the spiritual preconscious by means of a spiritualised emotion.

## Poetic intuition as cognitive

As we have seen, Maritain maintains that poetic intuition is cognitive both of the reality of things and of the subjectivity of the artist. He explains what he means by that 'reality of things' which constitutes the object of poetic intuition. The word 'object' is equivocal in this case, he argues, for things are objectivised in a concept. Since there is no concept in poetic intuition, there can be no objectivisation. Poetic intuition therefore is not directed towards essences; these are the objects of speculative knowledge, being separated from reality in concepts and examined by means of reasoning. Poetic intuition, rather, 'is directed towards concrete existence as connatural to the soul pierced by a given emotion'.[14] Every time it operates it tends towards some concrete singular existent, grasping this existent in its passage through time in an attempt to immortalise it. Poetic intuition does not limit itself to this given existent, however, but because it does not possess any conceptualised object it goes infinitely beyond the existent, extending to all the infinite reality engaged in its existence. In other words, Maritain maintains, poetic intuition grasps the singular existent together with the other realities

14 Ibid., p. 126.

which are connected with it and echo within it; and all this resounds in the artist's subjectivity.[15]

For Maritain, poetic intuition is also cognitive in relation to the subjectivity of the artist, which it obscurely reveals. As we noted previously, both the thing grasped and subjectivity are known together in the same obscure experience. In addition, the thing grasped in poetic intuition is grasped only through its affective resonance in and in union with subjectivity. Poetic intuition, therefore, is filled with the subjectivity of the poet as well as with the thing grasped. It is clear that for Maritain the person is not just a mirror, but a living mirror whose affective life tinctures reality just as reality tinctures his life. Moreover, the grasping of things, together with the awakening of subjectivity to itself, is ordered towards the expression of the subjectivity of the artist in the work that issues from the creativity of the spirit. Of these two elements in poetic intuition the more immediate is the experience of external reality, since it is natural for the human soul to know things before coming to self-knowledge. The principal element, however, is the experience of the self. For it is only when subjectivity awakens to itself that emotion received in the spiritual preconscious of the intellect is made intentional and intuitive, that is to say, the instrument of knowledge through connaturality.

It follows from the foregoing, contends Maritain, that the artistic artifact is a revelation both the subjective and objective poles of experience – of the subjectivity of the artist and of whatever reality poetic knowledge delivers to him. It is an indissoluble unity, just like the poetic intuition from which it issues. Whatever the artistic medium (poetry, painting, music), in it alone is poetic intuition objectivised. As well as being an object in its own right, it is at the same time both a direct sign of the deeper aspects and relations ensconced in reality and a sign of the subjective world of the artist. Thus, posits Maritain, just as poetic intuition grasps things in their abundant significance, so too the artist's work abounds in meaning, pointing beyond itself and saying more than it is.

**15** Ibid.

---

## Conclusion

Maritain's use of the notion of knowledge through inclination or connaturality enabled him to formulate an aesthetic theory possessing much contemporary appeal. The problem is, however, that Aquinas did not develop any aesthetic theory, as we have seen, and he most certainly did not employ the notion of knowledge through connaturality in relation to artistic creativity. Eco believes that although it is possible to extend the notion of knowledge through connaturality to the domain of aesthetic experience, this cannot be done without adopting a typically modern position – by implication, a position with which a Thomist should be uncomfortable.[16] However, having proved to his own satisfaction that Maritain's theory of artistic creativity is historiographically and epistemologically ill-founded, he does not proceed – reasonably enough – to offer any critique of the use of this concept in Maritain's aesthetic theory.

It is our contention that the concept of knowledge through inclination is the soul that animates the whole of Aquinas' thought. If this belief is correct, then any authentically Thomistic aesthetic theory ought to take account of this notion. We will show that Maritain has not only unearthed a concept which is capable of accounting for developments in contemporary artistic practice, but that it is moreover a concept which can bear fruit when applied to the receptive phase of aesthetic experience, that is to say, aesthetic perception.

At this point, therefore, we turn to a consideration of the notion of knowledge through inclination in Aquinas' thought, drawing substantially upon Rafael-Tomás Caldera's magisterial exegetical study in order to guide us.

---

**16** *La definizione*, p. 122.

---

CHAPTER FIVE

# Knowledge through inclination

*The twofold manner of judging in the* Summa Theologiae

A T THE BEGINNING OF THE *Summa Theologiae*, Aquinas distinguishes between two manners of judging, namely judgment *per
modum cognitionis* and judgment *per modum inclinationis*:[1]

> Since judgment appertains to wisdom, there are two kinds of
> wisdom corresponding to *a twofold manner of judging*. A man
> may judge *in one way by inclination*, as whoever has the habit of
> virtue judges rightly of what ought to be done in accordance
> with it by his very inclination towards it. Hence it is said that
> the virtuous man is the measure and rule of human acts. *In
> another way, by a cognitive process*, just as a man learned in moral
> science can judge rightly about virtuous acts, though he himself
> lack virtue. The first manner of judging divine things belongs to
> that wisdom which is set down among the gifts of the Holy
> Ghost: 'The spiritual man judgeth all things' (1 *Cor.* 2: 15). And
> Dionysius says (*Div. Nom.* ii): 'Hierotheus was taught not by
> mere learning, but by undergoing the experience of divine
> things.' The second manner of judging belongs to this doctrine
> which is acquired by study, though its principles are obtained by
> revelation.[2]

---

**1** Aquinas also makes this distinction, albeit employing different terminology, in his
*Scriptum super Sententiarum* and *In librum beati Dionysii De Divinis Nominibus*. Since
his understanding of the distinction between two manners of judging is the same in these
two works as in the *Summa Theologiae*, we propose to confine ourselves to a consideration of the evidence of the latter.   **2** ST, 1, 1, 6 ad 3. My trans. My italics, except quotations from Scripture and *De. Div. Nom.* Aquinas makes the same distinction, albeit once
more employing slightly different terminology, in ST, 2–2, 45, 2: 'We have said that
wisdom implies a certain rectitude of judgment in accordance with divine norms. Now

In order to clarify the distinction he has made between the two different ways of judging Aquinas offers two examples taken from the natural realm of human action. On the one hand, the virtuous man judges with rectitude concerning that which ought to be done in accordance with virtue in so far as he is inclined to it (*inquantum ad illa inclinatur*). (Aristotle also asserts that the virtuous man is the measure and rule of human actions.)[3] On the other hand, the man who is learned in moral science can judge virtuous actions *per modum cognitionis* even if he himself is not a virtuous person. The principal difference emphasised by Aquinas between the two manners of judging concerns the rule or measure which is employed in each case. In the case of knowledge *per modum inclinationis*, the inclination of the virtuous man is invoked. In the case of knowledge *per modum cognitionis*, it is the intellectual knowledge concerning moral matters which furnishes the measure; this is so even when virtue is lacking in the case of the one who judges. It would be reasonable to posit the structures of these two types of judgment to be somewhat different from one another; however, apart from an allusion made in passing, namely that the virtuous man judges virtuous actions in so far as he is inclined to them, Aquinas does not develop this point. It is reasonable to conclude, however, that he considers both to be of equal validity since he refers to both in order to elucidate his understanding of wisdom.

rectitude of judgment can come about in two ways: *first, through the perfect use of reason* [*secundum perfectum usum rationis*]; *secondly, through a certain connaturality with the matter about which one has to judge* [*propter connaturalitatem quamdam ad ea de quibus jam est judicandum*]. Thus, in matters of chastity, one who is versed in moral science will come to a right judgment *through rational investigation* [*per rationis inquisitionem*], while he who has the habit of chastity judges of such matters *by a kind of connaturality* [*per quamdam connaturalitatem*]. So it is with divine things. A correct judgment made *through rational investigation* [*ex rationis inquisitione*] belongs the wisdom which is an intellectual virtue. But to judge aright *through a certain connaturality* [*secundum quamdam connaturalitatem*] with them belongs to that wisdom which is the gift of the Holy Spirit. Dionysius says in *De Div. Nom.* that Hierotheus is perfect in Divine things *for he not only learns about them but suffers them as well* [*non solum discens, sed et patiens divina*]. Now this sympathy or connaturality with Divine things results from charity, which unites us to God: *he who is joined to the Lord, is one spirit with him* (1 *Cor.* 6:17). Consequently wisdom which is a gift has its cause in the will, that is, charity, but is has its essence in the intellect, whose act is to judge aright, as stated above.' My italics, except quotations from Scripture and *De Div. Nom.*  **3** *The Nicomachean Ethics*, X, 5 (1176).

## *The notion of judgment* per modum inclinationis

The relevant passages in Aquinas indicate that affective inclination allows the realisation of a judgment, that is to say, the right determination of the object towards which one experiences a certain connaturality. It is on the basis of this inclination that the virtuous man is said to be the rule and measure of human actions. In a like manner the mystic is assimilated to God, the supreme rule, and so becomes capable of judging all things: the spiritual man judges all things (*spiritualis homo iudicat omnia*).[4] By his inclination, therefore, a virtuous man is constituted as a rule for the right determination of the object towards which he inclines. Indeed judgment *per modum inclinationis* is analogous both to judicial judgment and to judgment *per modum cognitionis*. In a judicial judgment the judge must consult the pertinent laws in order to be able to measure the object of dispute and the rightness or otherwise of the parties involved.[5] In judgment *per modum cognitionis* the definition of an object allows us to judge its properties. In the case of judgment *per modum inclinationis*, a man becomes the rule of virtuous actions by virtue of the inclination which he has in his affectivity. Indeed, by his love for God he becomes the supreme rule. Virtue renders him capable of discerning correctly the object of his inclination.

It is important to realise that this manner of judgment is not about the affective reaction; neither is it a judgment about the object. Understood precisely, judgment *per modum inclinationis* is a judgment *about* the object *by means of* the affective reaction of the subject. We may say, borrowing a formula proposed by Caldera (a formula which will require further justification), that judgment by inclination is *an intuitive judgment of the value of an object, posited by means of the affective reaction of the subject in relation to it.*[6]

That Aquinas means a kind of judgment when he speaks of knowledge through connaturality or affective knowledge is evident from the fact that this is the term which occurs in almost all the relevant texts.

---

4 1 *Cor.*, 2:15.  5 We assume for the sake of argument that the judge is just; otherwise he would be less capable of rendering just judgment on others, no matter how learned he might be in the law.  6 Rafael-Tomás Caldera, *Le jugement par inclination chez saint Thomas d'Aquin* (Paris, 1980), p. 68.

The term *cognitio affectiva*, which appears in some texts,[7] points to the intellectual character of affective knowledge. Judgment properly speaking means a measuring or right determination (*recta determinatio*) of the data; in this sense it is opposed to *perceptio* or *apprehensio*, a simple immediate grasp of the object. Of course, apprehension or perception is a necessary condition for judgment to take place, except in the case of judgment proper to the senses, where the two moments are identical. Consequently, affective knowledge or judgment *per modum inclinationis* does not constitute a privileged mode of apprehending the object.

## Knowledge and love

Affective knowledge is a synthesis of two moments which constitute the spiritual life of man, namely knowledge and love. In other words, it is the term of a synthesis of cognitive and volitional activity. Philosophical analysis, in an effort to deepen our understanding of the structure of human activity, can separate and isolate the various elements which constitute the integrity of that activity. In reality, however, these elements are inseparable in the concrete unity of the human person. Thus, there is no love without knowledge, and there is no knowledge without love.

The human soul is a unity. We can say therefore that as a principle of operation, it is also one. In its operation, however, it is not one but manifold. In the words of Ignazio Camporeale, 'knowledge and love differ in so far as they are activities, while they are identical in the principle from which they proceed and the end to which they tend'.[8] The human soul is in fact the single principle of different and distinct operations which are differentiated from one another by the way they reach their object. The dynamism which establishes a relation between the unicity of the subject and the unicity of the object, between consciousness and reality, is manifold and subject to variation. Nonetheless, even though the cognitive and volitional activities of the soul constitute distinct operations, they are indivisibly unified in their principle.

7 See ST, 2–2, 97, 2 ad 2; ST, 2–2, 162, 3 ad 1; ST, 1, 64, 1.   8 Ignazio Camporeale, 'La conoscenza affettiva nel pensiero di S. Tommaso', *Sapienza* 12 (1959), 256.

In *De Potentia* Aquinas conceives this synthesis of love and knowledge in terms of a circular movement which has its point of departure in the thing itself going to the subject and thence returning to the thing in itself: 'We receive our intellective knowledge from external things: and by our will we tend to something external as an end.'[9] The external good moves the intellect, the intellect moves the will and the will tends towards the external good. This image of circularity impresses upon us the reciprocity of influence between knowledge and love. While they are each distinct from one another, at the same time they end and develop in one another.

Camporeale points out that since every reality is one in itself (*unum per se*), if it is to be grasped in its totality and unity it must perforce be attained at the same time as *true* and as *good*. Consequently, it must simultaneously be known and loved. 'Unless the appetibility of a reality is grasped in its intelligibility and its intelligibility is grasped in its appetibility, the being of the object in its unity and totality will always in some way escape the subject.'[10] Knowledge of the object will be perfect only if it takes place in the very love of the object. The necessity of affective knowledge thus becomes clear.

We can apply the same line of reasoning to the subject since he is also a unitary composite being. The first principle of operation of the human soul is one, even though we can discern distinct moments in its activity by means of abstraction. These diverse aspects of its dynamism must therefore form a perfect synthesis in concrete reality. The subject, in so far as he exists, is one. Consequently, he is also one in the concrete reality of his operation.

The spiritual activity of man is a synthesis of knowledge and love. The individual human subject does not first know and then love: we employ these abstract distinctions of before and after in order the better to analyse human activity. Human activity is in fact complete in itself at every instant. In concrete reality all its different operations are involved in a perfect synthesis which philosophical analysis finds difficult to grasp. In actual reality all love involves knowledge and all knowledge involves

9 *De Potentia*, 9, 9.  10 Camporeale, 'La conoscenza affettiva', 257.

love. This conclusion supports our contention that moral knowledge involves a synthesis of both knowledge *per modum inclinationis* and knowledge *per modum cognitionis.*

It is this very unity in the human composite which explains, moreover, why the intense exercise of one particular power impedes in whole or in part the exercise of the others. As Aquinas explains, all the powers of the soul are grounded in its one single essence. Thus if the soul's energies are vigorously employed in the activity of one power, they must be withdrawn from the activity of any other power.[11] It is this unity in the human composite which also explains why the passions of the sensible appetite can impact on the will. A man's disposition can be changed by a passion of the sensible appetite. Thus an action may appear good to a man when he is in a rage, though this would not be the case if he were composed.[12] Similarly, spiritual joy or sadness can affect the body and its various sensible functions.[13]

The immediate presence of affective reaction to consciousness is therefore a consequence of the ontological unity of the human subject. This immediate presence allows us to know our affective reactions without the necessity of recourse to further reflection. For affections are rather in intelligence as in their principle and source, where there is a certain notion of them. They are as a thing caused in its principle, which contains some notion of the thing caused.[14] This means in effect that we enjoy direct experimental knowledge of affective reactions which are grasped by consciousness without the mediation of reasoning, just as 'we perceive the will in the act of willing, and life in vital activity'. For 'what is in the soul by essential presence is known *by experiential knowledge*'.[15]

## *The role of* habitus *in judgment* per modum inclinationis

The term *habitus* denotes 'a definite ability for growth through activity'.[16] This ability for growth through activity does not belong to the

---

**11** ST, 1–2, 37, 1.  **12** ST, 1–2, 9, 2.  **13** ST, 1–2, 38, 4 ad 3.  **14** ST, 1, 87, 4 ad 3.  **15** ST, 1–2, 112, 5 ad 1. My italics.  **16** Romanus Cessario OP, *The moral virtues and theological*

orders of creation below man, for they are determined in their operations. They are definitely fixed by their form and so lack that absence of
determination necessary for the development of habit.[17] The human soul
is a true subject of habit since in it is found an element of receptivity and
potency, and it is the principle of a number of different operations. It
thus fulfils the conditions required for the development of habit.[18]

Aquinas conceives of *habitus* as a quality: it does not pertain to the
very substance of man; it is rather a definite disposition added to and
modifying it. For scholastic theologians it has an important role to play
in shaping human conduct. They describe *habitus* as mediating between
potency and actuality. Gilson expresses this notion very well when he
states that the characteristic feature of habit is that 'it is a disposition of
the subject in reference to his own nature'. In other words, 'the habit of
a being determines the manner in which he realises his own definition'.[19]

As a consequence of the fact that habit determines the manner in
which a subject realises himself, the notion of the good is an integral part
of its description. The reason for this is quite clear. Every being is what
it is on account of its form. Form necessitates a certain orientation of the
subject towards its end and the notion of end is correlative with the
notion of goodness. In so far as habit facilitates a subject in attaining to
an end which contributes to his realisation as a human being, therefore,
it is a good habit. In so far as it impedes this realisation, it is a bad habit.
*Habitus* can therefore be defined in general as the disposition according
to which a subject is well- or ill-disposed. More than a simple disposition, however, *habitus* denotes a certain stability. Since habits have stable
causes, they cannot easily be lost. Such are the habits of virtue and of science.[20]

---

*ethics* (Notre Dame, 1991), p. 34.  **17** Angels are the subjects of habits, but these are analogous to human habits. This is because there is no potentiality of matter in angels,
although there is some potentiality in them – for to be pure act is proper to God alone.
To the extent that potentiality is found in them, they are the subjects of habits. It remains,
however, that the potentiality of matter and the potentiality of an intellectual substance
are not of the same kind. Consequently, the habits of men and angels are different from
one another. See ST, 1–2, 50, 6.  **18** ST, 1–2, 49, 4.  **19** *The philosophy of St Thomas
Aquinas* (New York, 1929), p. 312.  **20** ST, 1–2, 49, 2 ad 3.

Our concern here of course is the *habitus* of virtue. The virtuous man, that is to say, the subject of good habits in the practical domain, is the rule and measure of human actions and can judge *per modum inclinationis*. He makes such a judgment in so far as he is inclined towards the object of his virtue (*inquantum ad illa inclinatur*)[21] or through a certain connaturality with it (*per quamdam connaturalitatem ad ipsa*).[22] Both these notions refer of course to affectivity. Our concern here is to examine the role of *habitus* in this kind of judgment, or rather how the mediation of *habitus* is realised in judgment.

Commenting on Aristotle's *Nicomachean Ethics*, Aquinas states that the virtuous person correctly passes judgment on individual things that pertain to human activity because in each particular case that which is truly good appears to him to be good. Aquinas explains that this is so 'because things seem naturally pleasurable to each habit that are proper to it, that is to say, agree with it'. In the case of the habit of virtue, those things which are agreeable to it are in fact good because moral virtue is defined by what is in accord with right reason. 'Thus', says Thomas, 'the things in accord with right reason, things of themselves good, seem good to it.'[23] Following Aquinas' lead, Caldera says of the virtuous man that 'his virtue puts him in harmony with the true good since virtue consists in this harmony'.[24]

We encounter the same doctrine in the ST, 2-2, 24, 11. Here Aquinas explains that just as the sense of taste discerns tastes according to its habitual disposition, so too man judges the object of his actions according to his habitual disposition. This is so because habit makes what is agreeable to him seem good, and what is repugnant to him seem bad.[25] Habit there-

---

**21** ST, 1, 6 ad 3. **22** ST, 2–2, 45, 2. **23** *In Ethic.*, III, lectio X (no. 494). **24** Caldera, *Le jugement par inclination*, p. 75. **25** In response to the charge of relativism – that is *really* good which *seems* to me to be good – let us direct the reader to a metaphysical account of the good. (See for instance Caldera, 'Le discernement du bien', in *Le jugement par inclination*, 31–58.) As always, Aquinas steers a *via media* between objectivism and subjectivism. The ontological constitution of an object is such that it is good in so far as it is perfect, and this is so independently of human apprehension. A habit will incline a faculty to that which is truly good in so far as the habit itself is proportioned to the good; it will incline the faculty to that which is lacking in goodness in so far as it lacks due proportion to the good: such as a man is, so does his end appear to him (*qualis*

fore makes that which is in agreement with itself seem good. This is so even in the case of evil, when the habit of the subject is a vice and not a virtue.[26]

The mediation of habit in the discernment of good is a constant in Aquinas' doctrine concerning judgment in moral matters.[27] Aquinas constantly describes the manner of this discernment as an intuitive judgment analogous to the judgment of the senses or, again, analogous to the intellect's discernment of the first principles of speculative reason.[28] Thus, whatever is in agreement with a person's habit appears spontaneously to him as good, and whatever is repugnant to it appears spontaneously to him as bad. It is precisely the integration of affectivity in the process of discernment which renders judgment spontaneous and which also explains the frequent analogy which Aquinas draws between judgment *per modum inclinationis* and the senses.[29]

## Choice

Having examined the role of *habitus* in knowledge *per modum inclinationis*, we now propose to examine another aspect of action, namely *choice*, that is, the adherence of the will to the good. Philosophical analy-

---

*unusquisque est, talis finis videtur ei*, ST, 1–2, 9, 2). The objective ontological constitution of the object, however, remains unaffected by human apprehension. The goal of the moral life, when viewed in these terms, is to achieve a right proportion between our internal subjective constitution and the objective constitution of external reality. **26** See ST, 2–2, 59, 2. **27** 'That a person well defines something in matters of virtuous action issues from the habit of virtue, thus a chaste person decides aright on issues affecting chastity'. ST, 2–2, 60, 1. **28** See ST, 2–2, 2, 3 ad 2. **29** Benoît Garceau argues that, from a Thomistic perspective, the primary analogue of judgment could be considered to be that of well-disposed sense-faculties. Referring to the judgment of the just judge, he states that 'if, for him [Aquinas], the primary analogue of the virtue of justice pertains to acts of the virtue of justice, this perhaps is only a primary semantic analogue. The notion of judgment was drawn from the domain of justice and came to designate any right determination of an object – as much in speculative as in practical matters. It could be, however, that from a Thomistic perspective the true primary analogue of judgment – that of the virtue of justice as much as that of the virtues of temperance and fortitude – is the *discernment* by well-disposed senses of their proper objects': *Judicium: vocabulaire, sources, doctrine de saint Thomas d'Aquin* (Paris, 1968), p. 229.

---

sis demands that we separate judgment (an act pertaining to the intellect) and choice (an act pertaining to the will) within the unitary reality of an action. Fidelity to the real, however, requires that we reconstitute them in their unity at the term of our analysis. The reality is that although judgment is an act of the intellect, judgment concerning the concrete good to be done here and now cannot be divorced from the dynamism of the will. Indeed, the intellect works on behalf of the will instead of exercising its activity for its own ends. Choice can quite legitimately be termed 'an appetitive reasoning'.30 When examining whether free will (*liberum arbitrium*) is a faculty of knowledge because it is called *quasi liberum iudicium*, Aquinas comments that judgment occurs at the end of deliberation. He tells us that the course of action to be taken is determined firstly by a proposition of the reason and secondly by its acceptance by appetite – as Aristotle says, '*having formed our judgment through the process of counsel we desire what we have decided*'. 'Thus', concludes Aquinas, 'choice is a kind of judgment, which is why it is called in Latin "free judgment"'.31 Choice can therefore be called *judgment* because it is a kind of final verdict on the object in question. As Caldera points out, action is in fact a synthetic whole, constituted by both knowledge and volition.32

Choice requires both an end desired by the subject and determination of the means necessary in order to attain that end. Unless the will have an end it cannot be moved and action is impossible; the will simply remains in potency. On the other hand, when the object of the will is totally determined there can be no question of choice either. Other means either do not exist or are simply excluded. In this case all that is required is for the will to cling to its object. Choice therefore supposes that the means required to attain the end stand in need of determination. The word *determination* must here be understood to mean not only that the best means to attain the end are determined by reason; the will must also adhere to these means. When the will thus adheres, choice can be said to have taken place.

**30** George P. Klubertanz SJ, *The philosophy of human nature* (New York, 1953), p. 242.
**31** ST, I, 83, 3 ad 2.   **32** Caldera, *Le jugement par inclination*, p. 117.

The structure end-means is therefore essential to choice. Choice could not exist without it. We should note that in the case of an action which is to be executed, every means is itself an end, albeit a proximate end, subordinate to the final end. It thus constitutes an object of deliberation and choice.

When the will clings to a particular means in order to realise a certain end, there is but one intention. Consequently, the action itself has a unitary character. In the words of Caldera, 'it is a synthetic act in which two elements are integrated in a single tension: the means are taken in the tension of the will towards the end'.[33] Thus Aquinas posits that 'when', for example, 'I say, "I am determined to take this medicine because I am determined to get well," I signify but a single motion of my will'.[34] When something is willed as a means to a goal, one and the same act of the will tends towards the goal and the means together; it moves towards the means required to attain the end, precisely because of and in its movement towards the end.

Basing himself on the foregoing observations, Caldera points out that choice depends on the ends sought by the subject. The expression 'end sought' is in fact crucially important, for it conceals all the subjectivity of the moral agent.[35] When a human subject measures the means to attain a certain end, his measuring is not simply based on a rational appraisal of the situation, for all his subjectivity is involved therein.

In establishing the facts of any particular situation, the subjectivity of the agent renders his attention selective. Our attention is limited and often it is not humanly possible to be aware of all the facts relevant to a particular situation. Consequently, the agent must make a choice concerning the importance or otherwise of the particular facts in question. This he does according to his own scale of values: he pays attention to what he regards as important and disregards what he deems to be unimportant. In other words, right from the very beginning the subject's deliberations concerning the possible object of action are already conditioned by the selection of data which he regards as relevant. Such as a man is,

33 Ibid. **34** ST, 1–2, 12, 4. **35** Our exposition is based on that of Caldera, *Le jugement par inclination*, pp 118ff.

so does his end seem to him (*qualis unusquisque est, talis finis videtur ei*).[36]

The data which one selects will be crucial to the outcome of one's deliberation. However, the virtuous man is able to achieve objectivity in his considerations because his selection of data faithfully mirrors, on a smaller scale, the complexities of the situation confronting him. A man's rightly ordered affectivity allows him to view reality without his intellect being obscured by disordered passions: 'The virtuous man is the rule and measure of all human actions, because in human affairs individual concrete actions are such as the virtuous man judges them to be".[37]

Because of his rightly ordered affectivity and his consequent heightened intellectual assessment of reality, the virtuous man is able to achieve objectivity in his consideration of the facts of any particular situation. His preferences are in accord with and a reflection of reality. The corrupt man, on the other hand, cannot achieve such objectivity. His disordered affectivity distorts his perception of the situation and so his selection of data does not reflect reality as it is. His selection of data is, rather, a construction of his own subjectivity. Affectivity therefore, when it reacts to the facts of a given situation, betrays the value system of the subject: he approves what he considers and considers what he approves. 'By a sort of self-economy the quality of the personality tends to reinforce itself: the subject finds what he wanted to find".[38]

A further observation about choice concerns the nonnecessity of arguments in relation to the movement of the will. A free act is not the fruit of a rational conclusion; rather, it cleaves to its object by virtue of a movement which it controls itself, in so far as it pertains both to the specification of the act and to its exercise. The only object necessary for the will in the order of specification is happiness or beatitude.[39] There is no good which compels necessary choice apart from total goodness, that is to say, the good which is good under every aspect. This state of affairs issues from the will's openness to goodness in all its universality on account of its rational nature. The will by its very essence tends towards the universal good; in reality, however, it is constantly confronted by par-

---

**36** ST, 2–2, 24, 11.  **37** *In Epistolam I ad Corinthios*, c. II, lect. II.  **38** Caldera, *Le jugement par inclination*, p. 119.  **39** See *De Malo*, 6, art. 1.

ticular goods. Since particular goods cannot satisfy its desire, they cannot constitute compelling ends for it. Consequently, the will remains totally free in respect of them.[40]

Choice is therefore neither a rational *conclusion* nor the conclusion of a *reasoning process*. Rather, as Caldera explains, 'it intervenes at the end of, or it *puts an end to* a process of deliberation where, in addition to all the rational considerations of the subject, the whole weight of subjectivity makes itself felt'. Since, moreover, deliberation must begin with a selection of the relevant data to be considered, its unfolding toward the point when choice takes place 'resembles a process of *increasing inclination* more than a reasoning process, a process which begins with the state in which the subject finds himself and proceeds towards that which, in short, attracts him the most'.[41] Benoît Garceau in expressing this idea says that in the final analysis judgment rests on the dynamism of human nature more than on a well-conducted rational examination of the relations obtaining between a particular rule and objects to be evaluated.[42]

In the act of choice, the will cleaves to the end by way of the means adopted. The act therefore receives its moral specification from the end. In other words, the end sought by the moral agent gives its form to the act. In choosing, the will moves towards a particular object because it realises (or leads to the realisation of) the final or ultimate end which the subject desires. Consequently, when a proximate or nonultimate choice is made, the object chosen is seen in and determined by the light of the final good. Thus, for example, when a person chooses to take a walk for the sake of his health, the project undertaken is obviously the walk. However, the object of the choice is a walk for the sake of his health. Here the end sought (health) is the final formal determination of the object of his choice.

It becomes clear therefore that true and false goods differ from one another in their ordering towards the final end. For man this final end and principal good is the enjoyment of God. A secondary good can be of two kinds, namely 'one which is truly good and by its nature capable

**40** See ST, 1–2, 10, 2.   **41** Caldera, *Le jugement par inclination*, p. 121.   **42** *Judicium: vocabulaire, sources, doctrine de saint Thomas d'Aquin*, pp 233–4.

of being directed to the principal good which is the ultimate end, another a seeming but not a true good, since it leads man away from his final good'.[43] Thus, it is to be noted that only an object capable of being ordered to the final good is a true good. This we believe has ramifications for what can be considered as being truly beautiful when considered in a Thomistic perspective, since the good and the beautiful are identical although conceptually different.

## The man learned in moral science who lacks virtue

The data which one selects in order to make a choice will be crucial to the outcome of one's deliberation. However, as we have seen, the virtuous man is able to achieve objectivity in his considerations because his selection of data faithfully mirrors on a smaller scale the complexities of the situation confronting him. For Aquinas, judgment *per modum inclinationis* is the most important source of illumination of the *intellectus illustratus*: a man's rightly ordered affectivity allows him to view reality without his intellect being obscured by disordered passions: 'The virtuous man is the rule and measure of all human actions, because in human affairs, individual concrete actions are such as the virtuous man judges them to be.'[44] Because of his rightly ordered affectivity and his consequent heightened intellectual assessment of reality, the virtuous man is able to achieve objectivity in his consideration of the facts of any particular situation. His preferences are in accord with and a reflection of reality. The corrupt man, on the other hand, cannot achieve such objectivity. His disordered affectivity distorts his perception of the situation and so his selection of data does not reflect reality as it is. His selection of data is, rather, a construction of his own subjectivity. When confronted with the facts of a given situation, therefore, a subject's affectivity colours his perception in such a way that his personal bias, whether good or bad, tends to reinforce itself.

In order to conclude our discussion of knowledge *per modum inclinationis* in the thought of Aquinas, let us now return to his assertion that

**43** ST, 2–2, 23, 7.   **44** *In Epistolam I ad Corinthios*, c. II, lect. II.

---

'a man may judge ... *by a cognitive process*, just as a man learned in moral science can judge rightly about virtuous acts, though he himself lack virtue'.[45] We have argued that in any individual there is a synthesis of the rational and affective aspects of the human person: all knowledge is informed to some degree by affectivity, and all affectivity is informed by knowledge. This synthesis results from the ontological unity of the person. It is on account of this unity that knowledge and affectivity are mutually informing, each impacting on the other to varying degrees depending on the personality of the subject and the circumstances in which he finds himself.

The disordered affective 'keyboard' of the man who is learned in moral science, yet who lacks virtue, can lead only to a perception of moral reality which is likewise distorted. He considers what he approves and approves what he considers. The self-economy which we previously mentioned is as much operative in his case as in that of anybody else. It seems to me therefore that Aquinas' description of 'a man learned in moral science' as one who 'can judge rightly about virtuous acts, though he himself lack virtue' is not wholly accurate. A man who possesses a disordered affective structure necessarily suffers from an impaired vision of reality, for the ontological unity of the human person means that affectivity informs that vision, and *vice versa*. If we accept that 'reality is the foundation of ethics',[46] then we must conclude that the judgment of an ethicist lacking in virtue is erroneous to some extent, depending on the degree to which vice regulates his lifestyle.

We believe that the conclusions which we have drawn concerning the man learned in moral science who nonetheless lacks virtue, follow logically from the principles encountered in Aquinas' own thought. Aquinas, in ST, 1, 1, 6 ad 3 and in 2–2, 45, 2, distinguishes between knowledge *per modum inclinationis* and knowledge *per modum cognitionis*. This distinction is in effect for the sake of analysis for, as we have seen, these two modes of knowledge are always integrated in the individual. Any characterisation of knowledge *per modum cognitionis* which is divorced

---

**45** ST, 1, 1, 6 ad 3.   **46** Josef Pieper, *Living the truth: the truth of all things and the reality of the good*, trans. Lothar Krauth and Stella Lange (San Francisco, 1989), p. 111.

from knowledge *per modum inclinationis* – and *vice versa* – can function only as a theoretical construct which has nothing corresponding to it in actual reality. To say this, however, is not to diminish the importance of such a distinction. For it is only in examining the various elements of distinctions like this one that we can come to a more profound under-standing of the human person, so long as we reunite these various ele-ments at the term of our analysis.

## *Poetic knowledge as a specific form of knowledge* per modum inclinationis

In our outline of Maritain's theory of art, we have seen that he regards poetic knowledge as a specific form of knowledge through inclination or connaturality. Arising in a preconscious manner, it emerges into con-sciousness as a synthesis of emotion and intelligence. Since it is unable to issue in an internal concept, it issues instead in an external work. Indeed, opines Maritain, poetic knowledge is fully expressed only when it issues in a work. (Nonetheless, he does subscribe to the notion that it is possible to experience insights afforded by poetic intuition yet lack the technical wherewithal which would allow one to express those insights in the form of aesthetic artifacts.)

According to Maritain, the form of knowledge through connatural-ity proper to poetic knowledge is specified by way of emotion. Viewed in the light of our exposition of the notion of knowledge through incli-nation or connaturality in the thought of Aquinas, this contention appears to be unobjectionable. As we ascertained during the course of this exegesis, judgment by inclination or connaturality denotes *an intu-itive judgment of the value of an object, effected by means of the affective reaction of the subject in relation to it.*[47] Aquinas, of course, employs the notion of judgment through inclination only in relation to the moral and mystical domains of human experience. However, since poetic intu-ition itself involves an intuitive judgment in relation to an object by

[47] Caldera, *Le jugement par inclination*, p. 68.

means of the affective reaction which the subject experiences in relation to it, one can cogently argue that judgment *per modum inclinationis* also operates in the domain of aesthetic experience.

Intuitive judgment of value is one of the principal dynamic forces in everyday life: faced with persons, objects or situations we instinctively pass value judgments. These value judgments are realised without the mediation of a reasoning process properly speaking. The particular object in question gives rise to an instinctive reaction in the subject according as its mode of presence in him plays upon his affective constitution, the existence of which is evidenced by affective reactions. To deny that this notion can be properly applied to one whole domain of human experience, namely poetic intuition, in which intuitive judgments of value are posited, does appear to be somewhat arbitrary.

For Maritain knowledge through inclination, in so far as it is applied to poetic knowledge, is not merely emotional. This is because although it is effected through the instrumentality of feeling, it issues from the intellect precisely as intellect. This view also concurs with our understanding, arrived at on the basis of our examination of Aquinas' texts, of the notion of knowledge through inclination. Maritain argues that it is the intellect, and not emotion, that knows. He posits that emotion is received into the vital inner recesses of intelligence where it is transformed into an instrument of intelligence judging through inclination or connaturality. Thus, argues Maritain, in so far as it pertains to this process of knowledge through connaturality between subjectivity and reality, emotion determines intelligence in its preconscious activity, in a non-conceptual manner.

Our own investigation of the concept in Aquinas' texts also points to the intellectual character of affective knowledge: apprehension or perception is necessary for affective knowledge or judgment *per modum inclinationis* to take place. Consequently, judgment *per modum inclinationis* does not constitute a privileged mode of apprehending the object. Indeed, affective knowledge can be described as a synthesis of two moments in the life of the human person, namely knowledge and love; in other words, it is the term of a synthesis of cognitive and volitional activity. The philosophical foundation for this synthesis is found, on the one hand, in the ontological unity of the object which is known and loved and, on the other hand, in the existential unity of the human subject who thinks and loves. As we have argued, the spiritual activity of the human subject, when viewed in all its extension and integrity, is a synthesis of knowledge and love. All love involves knowledge and all knowledge involves love.

Maritain speculates at length on how the notion of knowledge through connaturality operates at the heart of artistic creativity; we argue that it applies equally in our perception and experience of beauty, a claim which is of greater import than that of Maritian since we are all conditioned with respect to how and even what we perceive as being beautiful.

CHAPTER SIX

# Knowledge through inclination and experience of beauty

WE HAVE CONSISTENTLY EMPHASISED in our deliberations that the human person is a unitary composite being. Thus, although we talk about intellect and will, for instance, there is in fact no knowing which does not involve the operation of the will and, *vice versa*, there is no willing which does not involve the operation of the intellect. Applying this notion to aesthetic experience, we can say that pleasure and displeasure do not belong to the same logical category as 'seeing', remembering, imagining and so on. Thus, for example, we cannot conceive ourselves taking pleasure in an object *instead* of 'seeing' it, remembering it, imagining it and so on. Pleasure therefore is not a distinct manner of experiencing things. It is rather a constitutive element in our very experience of things. We are aware of the pleasure which we experience in perceiving something beautiful. This pleasure, however, is not a distinct state of consciousness; it is rather an intrinsic part of the state of consciousness itself.

One major flaw in Eco's – and by extension, of the sources upon which he draws – exegesis of Aquinas' understanding of the aesthetic *visio* is his failure to take account of the implications of the fact that pleasure is an intrinsic part of the state of consciousness itself. While his delineation of Aquinas' account of various aspects of the life of mind – such as abstraction – is in itself without fault, he is guilty of divorcing Aquinas' exposition of these aspects from the latter's overall treatment of human nature. In terms of Eco's account, while the act of abstraction and judgement are indeed logically but not chronologically prior to the response of pleasure, the affective constitution of the individual does not enter into the workings of the mechanics of mind. In short, he fails to recognise that for Aquinas the emotions are part of the very warp and woof of the life of mind. His conception of the proportion between the intellect and its object is therefore informed by the Enlightenment fallacy that reason is free from any kind of conditioning factor whatsoever, a fallacy completely discredited by Gadamer and also well described by MacIntyre. For those who accept this critique, it is of the essence of rationality that its objectivity is inseparable from its freedom from the partialities of the various communities into which it finds itself thrown. MacIntyre informs us that 'It is to allegiance to reason as such, impersonal, impartial, disinterested, uniting, and universal, that the encyclopaedist summons his or her readers and hearers'.[1] MacIntyre, re-echoing Gadamer (albeit seemingly unconsciously), rejects this conception of reason, a rejection which coheres with our own interpretation of Aquinas on this same issue. MacIntyre also rebuts another false notion whereby reason is seen as 'the unwitting representative of particular interests, masking their drive to power by its false pretensions to neutrality and disinterestedness'.[2] Such a conception is of course completely alien to Aquinas as well; for Aquinas the object of the speculative intellect is the truth of things while the practical intellect, which is an extension of the speculative, translates into action the demands which arise from the very structure of reality itself. Fidelity to the real is at the heart of Aquinas' ethics, an ethics which therefore claims a universal extension.

According to MacIntyre there is a third possibility which holds that 'reason can only move towards being genuinely universal and impersonal in so far as it is neither neutral nor disinterested'.[3] Such conditioning, which is provided by membership of a particular type of moral community, one which excludes fundamental dissent, is 'a condition for genuinely rational enquiry'.[4] This is precisely the kind of context which Aquinas envisages for the unfolding of the life of mind. For him, as we have seen, 'custom (*consuetudo*) becomes a second nature, and produces an inclination similar to a natural one'.[5] In making this assertion, Aquinas

---

[1] Alasdair MacIntyre, *Three rival versions of moral enquiry: encyclopaedia, genealogy, and tradition* (Notre Dame, IN, 1990), p. 59.  [2] Ibid.  [3] Ibid., 59–60.  [4] Ibid., 60.  [5] ST, 1–2, 58, 1. As Clifford J. Kossel notes, we witness here a progression from *consuetudo* to *habitus*. Clifford G. Kossel SJ, 'Natural law and human law (Ia IIae, qq. 90–97)', in *The Ethics of Aquinas*, ed. Stephen J. Pope (Washington, DC, 2002).

recognises that reason cannot escape the influence of the social practices which furnish the context in which it necessarily operates. What are the implications of this assertion for a genuinely Thomistic theory of aesthetic perception?

The forms of community in which we participate condition in a fundamental way (speculative) reason's perception of what constitutes the human good. Family, friends and social institution have a fundamental bearing on our development as intellectual and moral agents. W. Jay Wood tells us that 'What goals are worth pursuing, what goals should be subordinated to others, what practices ought to be avoided and which pursued, and what resources are available to assist us in moral and intellectual growth are matters shaped in large measure within families, churches, schools and other social frameworks.' Thus, he continues, the complexion of one's intellectual life would vary considerably according as one were 'alternately a part of traditions whose chief goals were world economic domination, the biblical concept of shalom, aesthetic sensitivity, the dissolution of the self and union with God'.[6] One way in which this conditioning takes place is by way of inculcating a general configuration on the emotional structure of the individual, which structure we have argued is integral to the workings of the life of mind. While certain human emotions are universal, different emotions are differently shaped by different societies.[7] This shaping takes place by way of emotion labelling and normative evaluation, which labelling and evaluation enter into the content of the emotions that members of any particular society will experience.

The influence between emotion and reason is not unilateral; the operation of reason, as we have already argued, conditions ones emotional responses. At a very general level religion, metaphysics, philosophy and science make a great difference to the emotional life, as Nussbaum rightly observes. They not only provide a framework for understanding our world,

---

**6** W. Jay Wood, *Epistemology: becoming intellectually virtuous* (Leicester, 1998), 20. **7** For an in-depth discussion of the role of society in the formation of the emotions, see Martha Nussbaum, *Upheavals of thought: the intelligence of the emotions* (Cambridge, 2001), 139–73. **8** Ibid., p. 147.

but the nature of this framework shapes the emotions. Thus, points out Nussbaum, 'anger is shaped by views about who is responsible for what, and how the causality of evil works. Fear is shaped by thoughts about what harmful agencies exist in the world, how harmful they are, and how to ward them off.'[8] But each individual will experience his emotional response in a unique way, a response informed by his unique experience and knowledge. This uniqueness of response extends to the realm of the aesthetic, a fact which a reading of Aquinas as espousing a form of 'pure' reason expressed in Aristotelian categories fails to recognise.

But this is not all. For the individual is not completely constrained by the cultural horizons of his surroundings. As MacIntyre tells us, man is a 'culture-transcending dependent rational animal'. Thus, the individual is capable of pursuing an educational trajectory which enables him to transcend those aspects of his native culture which do not accord with the truth of the human condition and which therefore do not facilitate its objective flourishing.[9] The point is that on the part of any particular individual there is a constellation of factors which forge his unique perception of reality. With regard to experience of the emotions in particular, human beings are not shaped simply by social norms; individual history plays a vital role.

If we now return to Aquinas' definition of beautiful things as 'those things which when seen give pleasure', we will begin to appreciate that the conceptual tools which are to be found in his work allow for an infinite variety of aesthetic response to objects which are presented to human consciousness. At the most general level, each individual's experience of the object will betray the degree to which he is inserted within a given cultural community or group of communities. At the most particular level however there will in fact be as many varieties of experience of the object as there are individuals who behold it. Some species of experience will not qualify as aesthetic because the emotional constitution of the individual will prevent that 'seeing' which is necessarily constitutive of the aesthetic fact. In other cases some kind of intellectual appreciation

**9** An account of such an educational trajectory would, however, take us well beyond the confines of this chapter.

will take place, perhaps because education has facilitated it; the narrative history of the individual within the confines of his cultural experience, however, will serve to preclude that affective response which is also essential to the aesthetic *visio*. Such a person can have an intellectual appreciation but not an aesthetic experience of the object at hand. The one who find himself in this position views the object from the outside, as it were, for it is precisely love which unites the lover with the object of his love. While there is indeed an intellectual appreciation, it can rightly be question if there is real understanding. Real understanding requires that the human subject be connatured with the object of his perception; and such 'connaturing', as we have seen, is effected through a configuring of his affective structure in such a way that the contours of his understanding of the object are aligned with the objective constitution of the reality at hand. One might say that an appropriate emotional response is a necessary condition for that psychological proportion between subject and object which gives rise to the aesthetic *visio*.

Yet, on the other hand, pleasure in itself is not sufficient for aesthetic experience; that 'seeing' or intellectual apprehension, of which pleasure is integrally constitutive, must also be present. Indeed, given the unitary conception of the life of mind which we are adopting from Aquinas, we must say that a simple pleasurable response to an object, that is to say, a response which is uninformed by any intellectual 'seeing', is qualitatively different from pleasure which is intellectually informed. It ought to be borne in mind that the direction of influence between emotion and intellect is not simply one-way. Intellectual 'seeing' must also enter into the life of emotion and dictate what kind of ordering is appropriate for the object at hand in order for that object to become a source of aesthetic attraction. One must however avoid any simplistic intellectualist understanding which, maintaining a radical distinction between intellect and emotion, would hold that the informing of emotion by intellectual 'seeing' is sufficient for the aesthetic *visio*. As we have been at pains to point out, this 'seeing' is also a function of the affective state of the human subject.

## *Implications of knowledge through inclination for identifying and evaluating art*

There is a manifold complex of influences that goes to structure the emotional-intellectual life of any individual *qua* this unique individual. All individuals moreover experience and appropriate manifold complexes that are different at least to some degree from each other. There will however be areas of overlap which provide the basis for and which facilitate understanding between human beings. As Schleiermacher argues, 'everyone carries a tiny bit of everyone else within him, so that divination is stimulated by comparison with oneself'.[10] In other words, we share the same human nature, as Aristotle or Aquinas would say. It is precisely this reality which provides some basis for the interpretation of works of genius,[11] for aspects of our particular formation which we share in common with another enable us to enter to some degree into his life-world – in this instance as this life-world is symbolically expressed in the material conditions of the work of art. This entry, however, is possible only on the basis of the contours of affective response to a particular reality which we share in common with the other and without which, for the reasons already discussed, real understanding of what the other wishes to communicate is not possible. It is important however always to bear in mind that artists express themselves and their response to reality in shaping the materials of a medium of art. As Eldridge points out: 'In following that working of materials, we participate in the artist's attention, emotion, and expression'.[12]

Hence, just as the creation of a work of genius is not possible simply by following pre-established laws and rules, neither can a mechanical application of interpretative categories lead to an aesthetic response

---

**10** F. Schleiermacher. Quoted in Gadamer, *Truth and method*, p. 188.   **11** Such works are not produced mechanically according to already established laws and rules. Genius itself brings to light new models and rules. Thus, for example, literary genius uncovers previously unknown ways of employing language and new literary forms. It is precisely these kinds of developments that give rise to the possibility of communicating a qualitatively distinct, singular experience.   **12** Eldridge, *Introduction*, p. 204.

which is proportioned to the world of meaning which the artist has symbolically inscribed in the work of art. Schleiermacher would have employed the word 'congeniality' to denote this indispensable condition for true understanding. His usage bears an obvious similarity with the term 'connaturality' found in Aquinas and which provides a conceptual tool which is crucial for Maritain in his development of a theory of poetic intuition. Maritain talks about poetic knowledge as inseparable from the artist and his affectivity. We know on the one hand that it is precisely this kind of knowledge, coloured as it is by the emotional life of the subject, which is a necessary condition for that 'seeing' which is integral to the act of aesthetic perception. We are also aware on the other hand that a dynamic of reciprocity obtains between emotion and reason and that reason therefore is constitutive of the very quality of an emotional response. An actual effort to understand intellectually the work of art is thus necessary if one is to have access to that 'seeing' which issues from the subject in his psychophysical unity, that is to say that 'seeing' which is an intellectual-emotional synthesis. This understanding, as we intimated in the previous paragraph, cannot be separated from a grasp of the artist's shaping of materials, for these furnish the medium whereby we participate in his attention, emotion, and expression. Intellectual grasp and emotional response, while logically distinguishable, in fact constitute a hybrid reality which, in the case of aesthetic experience, is grounded in a response to the working of the materials of a particular artistic medium.

On account of the dynamic reciprocity that obtains between reason and emotion – although it is crucial to bear in mind that the relationship between them is one in which the former exercises a political rule over the latter – it is always possible for someone to develop a deeper appreciation of a work of art. This reciprocity, along with the discursive nature of reason and reason's relation to intellect, explains why aesthetic experience is narrative in structure. Indeed, this narrative structure explains why the very act of aesthetic appreciation contains virtually within itself a whole personal history which has led to this point in time. Only this unique personal history, this unique emotional and intellectual trajectory, can explain why one would 'see' the work of art in precisely the way one does and not in any other way. While the intentionality of emotion is a prerequisite for meaningful entry into the life-world of the artist as communicated in his work of art, it still remains that the emotional-intellectual history of each individual is unique. The implications of this point for aesthetic perception is clear: no two individuals can ever enjoy the same quality of aesthetic experience of a particular work. To say this is not to posit a comparison between these two different responses in the sense that one is better or worse than the other. Such a comparison is impossible since one is dealing with two incommensurable realities: the different emotional-intellectual trajectories create different existential perspectives from which each one 'sees' the object.

In making this point we do not wish to give the impression that a truly aesthetic response to an artifact is a universal experience for beholding subjects. It is always possible that the 'seeing' necessary for this experience does not take place in any particular instance. Let us explain. Given the unitary nature of human beings and the consequent fact that the intellect relies for its operation on the deliverances of the senses, the better disposed the senses are the greater will be the intellect's power of understanding.[13] Understanding – 'seeing' – is of course integral to the experience of beauty; not only, however, does such 'seeing' entail the emotions, it also depends on the sense faculties, as we know from our earlier outline of Aquinas' embryonic aesthetic theory. And it is always possible that factors pertaining to the senses, the emotions, or the intellect can undermine the possibility of that 'seeing' which is necessary for aesthetic experience.

It is precisely the different personal perspectives, conditioned by a person's intellectual-emotional trajectory as a body-soul composite in this life, which explain why it is possible for the beholder to appreciate the work of art in ways that might surpass in richness the appreciation of the artist himself. The artist has his own perspective on the truth that he attempts to embody in the work of art and, like all human perspec-

13 See ST, 1, 85, 7.

tives, it is limited. The unlimited number of perspectives from which the work can be viewed means that it is in potency to an unlimited number of realisations in terms of the aesthetic experience which it evokes in those who behold it. In saying this, we do not here wish to give the impression that we espouse some form of aesthetic relativism. Just as any human perspective on objective truth is limited and needs to be complemented by other appropriate perspectives, so also with regard to the experience of aesthetic value. With beauty we enter a realm which no limited human mind can hope to exhaust; all we can do is to behold its manifestations from different perspectives. There are moreover many different analogical instantiations of beauty: how does one compare the beauty of Chinese music with that of a canvass by Cézanne? Within the same medium, even within the same culture, beauty's concrete manifestation can take on wildly different forms. It would be a mistake therefore to think that because beauty has an objective status that we ought to be able to grasp it in its entirety and to reach complete unanimity in our judgements concerning it. Such would be a reductionist attitude, one which is quite alien to the Thomistic tradition.

## The problem of taste

On the basis of the foregoing deliberations, we can support Hume's view that in matters aesthetic, the standard of taste is established by the 'joint verdict' of those who are acknowledged as experts in the identification and evaluation of art.[14] Hume lists five criteria which are necessary for entry into the class of those deemed to be expert in art. Eldridge paraphrases and explicates these criteria:

> Strong sense is a matter of having a feel for what is plausible or implausible in a plot or in another treatment of a subject matter. Delicate sentiment is the ability to discern small-scale elements of a work and to note how their arrangement contributes to its

14 Hume is not clear whether it is a matter of consensus or of a majority.

success or failure. Practice in an art and its criticism, comparisons among works, and lack of prejudice are straightforwardly what they seem.[15]

Our account of the life of mind, however, contradicts the Enlightenment prejudice that such a thing as a lack of prejudice can exist. In the understanding we have advanced, some kind of bias is a prerequisite for any true aesthetic response to an object. Lack of prejudice bespeaks a dearth of emotional response, a kind of detachment which leaves one outside both the artistic artifact and the world which it communicates. Hume nevertheless has a point if by 'lack of prejudice' he means a transcending of ways of 'seeing' which are informed by a distorted affective structure. One might, for example, experience pleasure on regarding a work produced by one's own child and mistake this pleasure for that which would attend a truly aesthetic response to an artifact of real artistic value. In this kind of case an evaluation of an object according to its own merits is undermined. Kant is surely correct in viewing this sort of evaluation as an erroneous judgment of taste. In such a judgement, as Eldridge explains, 'what has happened is that one has misassessed and misreported the causal history of a pleasure one has felt. One has attended to the work in an interested way.'[16] Or as Aidan Nichols, when speaking about painting, puts it: 'The feelings we have, when these are other than a joy of the mind in the form embodied sensuously in the canvas, are extrinsic and posterior to that enjoyment which makes the experience an experience of the beautiful.'[17]

It seems reasonable to posit that those who are not attached in an interested way to an artifact and who possess the other qualities mentioned above are in a privileged position when it comes to evaluating works of art. It is counterintuitive to suggest that such qualities make no difference. In particular, the idea that a critic be formed within a tradition of art criticism is important, for not only will his powers of intel-

---

**15** Eldridge, *Introduction*, p. 167. **16** Ibid., p. 171. **17** Aidan Nichols OP, *The art of God incarnate: theology and image in Christian tradition* (London, 1980), p. 91.

lectual appreciation be enhanced, so too will his emotional responses – and these two elements are of course inseparable in the reality of 'seeing'. It is of course true that non-experts cannot tell independently of the verdicts of experts that the latter are correct in their judgements, a criticism which is directed at Hume's account of taste. We can perhaps see why this is inescapably so. Just as the virtuous man is the rule and measure of virtuous actions – and so virtue ethics gets embroiled in accusations of circularity – so too the true aesthete is the rule and measure of works of art. If it were possible to break out of the circularity involved here, it would also be possible for the aesthetically non-gifted to judge the evaluations of aesthetes simply by consulting relevant objective criteria. In being able to judge the evaluations of aesthetes though the aesthetically non-gifted would be at one and the same time aesthetes, for surely this judging would involve the ability to 'see' and indeed to 'see' from yet a higher perspective than the aesthetes who are judged. There is an obvious logical contradiction here.

What we have said about formation within a tradition of aesthetic criticism as a prerequisite for the kind of 'seeing' which is constitutive of aesthetic perception and the consequent superior aesthetic taste of some, on account of their native ability and their intellectual-emotional immersion in the tradition, does of course lead to the conclusion that we ought to defer to acknowledged experts in matters of art and beauty. In so doing we are more likely to cultivate the necessary subjective conditions for truly experiencing artifacts in a way which can count as genuinely aesthetic. When our personal narrative history reaches the point where we are able to 'see' aright, we can hardly be accused of being coerced by the judgements of others. We have become connatured with the object of our experience and thus our aesthetic response can be said to be autonomous. Paradoxically, however, this autonomy is possible only by insertion within a tradition. Just as virtue and law are mutually implicative notions, so too are aesthetic autonomy and received canons of aesthetic taste.[18] Heteronomy conduces to autonomy in matters of taste,

---

**18** See Kevin E. O'Reilly, 'The vision of virtue and knowledge of the natural law', *Nova et Vetera* 5 (2007), 41–65.

while the latter re-informs the canonical judgements which have been handed down by tradition. This assertion is in accord with Salim Kemal's interpretation of Kant on taste: 'Judgments of taste celebrate the relation of the individual to community, which is ever in process, for the individual's autonomous judgment is always in search of a warrant from the community, which is itself always in a process of development that depends on assent from its members'.[19]

Kant's approach to aesthetic taste is of course radically different from anything that might be termed Thomistic. Kant set out to solve the problem of aesthetic taste, that is to say, 'our capacity for responding to beauty'.[20] In doing so he attempted to synthesise the affective or emotive experiences of an individual and subjective faculty with the notion of universality, even necessity, in order to avoid aesthetic judgments being merely private and relativistic; otherwise beauty would be entirely in the eye of the beholder. In his theory he sought to resolve the antinomy between the individual and contingent functions of aesthetic taste, on the one hand, and the universal and necessary functions of taste, on the other. As Bredin and Santoro put it: 'He believed firmly that, although the experience of beauty is inevitably *my* subjective experience, unique to myself, I also expect and even demand that others should agree with my aesthetic judgements'.[21] This demand is based on the similarity in structure of the cognitive faculties of judging subjects.

A Thomistic explanation of the antinomy between the individual and contingent functions of aesthetic taste, on the one hand, and the universal and necessary functions of taste, on the other, can be found in Aquinas' unitary conception of human nature, in particular in the dynamic interplay between reason and emotion which is a consequence of this unity. According to Aquinas' philosophical realism, we can know things as they are. When faced with the same object, what two different people see is essentially the same thing; of this they are usually convinced on account of the philosophical realism that still informs normal daily living.

19 Salim Kemal, *Kant's aesthetic theory: an introduction* (New York, 1992), p. 99. 20 Ibid., 24. 21 Hugh Bredin and Liberato Santoro-Brienza, *Philosophies of art and beauty: introducing aesthetics* (Edinburgh, 2000), p. 80.

Nevertheless the emotional response which the object evokes in them may be radically different in each case. In both cases those intellectual processes described by Eco are operative. Because these intellectual processes are shared by all cognitive agents – barring of course some impediment to their functioning in some individual cases – and because they issue in universal concepts, it is quite easy to appreciate why judgements in matters aesthetic would have the 'feel' of universality if we bear in mind that we are not here dealing with 'pure' Kantian reason. In all experience of beauty reason is shot through with an emotional colouring; consequently, on judging an object as beautiful, a human subject will also be convinced, on account of the emotional grip to which this object gives rise, that all others should also deem it to be beautiful. Conversely, it is precisely this affective aspect of aesthetic experience which explains why others may very well not experience this object as being beautiful, while also believing their own personal experience to have universal extension.

## Art, morality and religion

Aquinas was not of course concerned with the values communicated by means of aesthetic artifacts; this phenomenon had not in his time been raised to the level of explicit consciousness. The notion of connaturality nevertheless furnishes a conceptual tool which enables us to develop an interpretation of proportion which extends beyond that of sense faculty to sense object and of 'pure' (emotionless) intellect to intellectual object. Aesthetic perception, according to a proper understanding of the principles found in Aquinas' thought, as we have seen, can never be simply a function of an intellectual reconstruction of the productive process. The cultural and personal horizons of the artist enter into the constitution of the aesthetic artifact, while the aesthetic *visio* (understood in its proper, holistic sense) of the beholding subject – conditioned as it is by his own cultural and personal horizons – in actualising the conditions of beauty of the object itself, also as it were colours them as well as being itself in turn coloured by them.

We ought not to forget that just as there is a dynamic interplay between emotion and intellect which conditions the way in which we 'see' an aesthetic artifact, so too there is a dynamic interplay between subject and artifact itself. Not only does the subject actualise the aesthetic potentialities in the artifact in a way which is proportioned to his capacity to 'see', so too does the artifact insert itself into his narrative history and influence the manner of its unfolding by the way in which it engages his intellect and emotion. In so doing it opens up certain future possibilities of 'seeing' and closes off others. A powerful aesthetic experience can alter the meaning of one's experience to date and influence the meaning of this experience as it subsequently develops. This is because the one who has been thus affected comes to inhabit 'by means of a communion of sympathy'[22] the world of meaning carried by the artwork

Intrinsically linked with the foregoing is the fact that any artwork enshrines its own set of values or disvalues – religious, moral, social, political, cultural – or, more precisely, it enshrines those of the artist, some of which he is conscious, others of which he is unconscious. Artifacts are in effect revelatory, that is to say, they are privileged loci in which values are distilled and by means of which they are communicated to others. Adapting slightly the words of Aidan Nichols we could say that values are 'not projected on to an arrangement of paints or of masses of stone'; they are rather 'already embodied and communicated there' through the creator's handling of the sensuous.[23] And values, by definition, can never be neutral; they can never be a matter of indifference. The problem that confronts us with regard to art, however, is that we are never presented simply with values. These values are always ensconced in the material conditions of the medium in which they are communicated, and the very allure of these conditions can facilitate the transmission and adoption, perhaps unconscious, of (dis)values on the part of the experiencing subject, (dis)values perhaps heretofore alien to his religious, moral, social, political, or cultural make-up. A work of art invites us to 'dwell in the experience'[24] which it offers; and we never remain uninfluenced or

---

**22** Nichols, *The art of God Incarnate*, p. 113.  **23** Ibid., p. 91.  **24** This phrase is taken from David Pole, *Aesthetics, form and emotion*, ed. G. Roberts (New York, 1983), p. 11.

unchanged by a genuine experience. In this view it is not just poetry that can corrupt; corruption lies within the capability of all the arts. A modern Plato would perhaps banish all the arts from society and not limit himself simply to poetry. The point is that it is simplistic in the extreme to ignore the role which artworks can play in the transmission and formation of values, and it is naïve if not irresponsible on the part of those entrusted with leadership roles within society not to cultivate the production of art which conduces toward the kinds of values which facilitate political, social, religious, moral, and cultural flourishing. That kind of art ought to be promoted which moves us, as Nichols tells us, to 'the suppression of self so that fidelity to ultimate values may replace the distortions of the relentless ego, so that the revelatory event proves able to place us in touch with an absolutely satisfying and complete hold on the reality that blesses us with its own truth, even if it calls on us for a painful reshaping of our lives'.[25]

The objection ought inevitably to arise that many great works of art obviously do not orient us one iota toward ultimate values. This assertion is undeniably true. Their worth consists in the fact that they distil and communicate the disvalues of a particular culture or age in their own unique and powerful way. Deep 'appreciation' of such works requires that one inhabit the world which they communicate, but such indwelling might perhaps be possible only by dulling the light of grace in one's life. The light of grace itself would dislodge the 'communion of sympathy' which would render such a work beautiful for the beholder, transporting him into another realm where the disvalues which the artwork communicates no longer exercise any attraction for him. The artwork in question simply gives him a window onto a reality which is divorced from true reality, albeit one which may well be to a greater or lesser extent the order of the day. Since man's own essence is part of the reality that confronts him, it too is distorted in his own perception of himself and so what Gabriel Marcel observed remains true, namely that 'contemporary art, in certain of its most disconcerting expressions, constitutes an

Quoted in Eldridge, *Introduction*, p. 202. **25** Nichols, *The art of God Incarnate*, p. 113.

irrecusable testimony of what must be called an alienation'.[26] By 'alienation' Marcel means the 'fact that man seems to have become more and more a stranger to himself, to his own essence – to the point of calling his essence into question, of refusing it at the very least all original reality'.[27] An artwork which comes into existence by means of an act animated by the mind of one who has placed himself to some degree or other outside the kind of mindset which is conditioned by belief in God may well boast great aesthetic worth and thus be of great cultural significance; it can nevertheless not lay claim to objective beauty. For it is important to remember that for our own times, what has aesthetic worth is not necessarily beautiful and whatever is beautiful does not necessarily have aesthetic worth. Only in the one who 'sees' with the eyes of faith do the aesthetic and the beautiful combine. Creation and appreciation of truly beautiful art, as we will see in the next chapter, can be the fruit only of a life lived under the influence of ultimate values.

The logic which we have pursued here does however present a difficult problem when we consider that many great works of religious art have been produced by non-believers. Consider, for example, Fauré's *Requiem*, or Matisse's chapel at Vence, of which Pie-Raymond Régamey says: '[It] has such an atmosphere in it that priests saying mass there have remarked that they have not offered the sacrifice with more fervour since their ordination.'[28] Can it really be that 'in certain cases a "non-Christian" will have a deeper, more genuine, and more effective feeling for the theme or function of a work than will a "Christian"?[29] Perhaps

26 Gabriel Marcel, *Problematic man*, trans. Brian Thompson (New York, 1967), pp 17–18.
27 Ibid., p. 18. Marcel continues: 'Everything is as if art, in a Picasso for example, came to manifest – I mean to make manifest – the deformed and as it were unrecongnizable image which the inner mirror reflects to us. For it is difficult seriously to admit that this deformation be obtained arbitrarily, that it be but the product of a deliberate and as it were perverse activity, or merely of what is sometimes called the "ludic" consciousness, that is, such as is exercised in play and without any utilitarian preoccupation. It is far more plausible to admit that we are in the presence of a profound need, which is that of objectifying what I will designate by a term purposefully vague, namely, existential modalities which are situated below the level of day-to-day consciousness' (ibid.). 28 Pie Raymond Régamey, *Religious art in the twentieth century* (New York, 1963), p. 178. 29 Ibid., p. 224.

it is necessary to recall that the artwork embodies meaning in sensuous form. Thus, while one artist might possess a profound and well-informed Christian belief, his powers to give expression to this belief in the shaping of sensuous form may be quite limited. Such art, needless to say, cannot be considered great. On the other hand, how do we explain the ability of great artworks by non-believers to communicate religious truths in a profoundly meaningful way? For to truly understand religious truths in this kind of way requires that one live them so that they become part and parcel of one's very being. In other words, a 'communion of sympathy' – that knowledge by connaturality in which love opens up new and hitherto unimagined vistas of 'seeing' – is indispensable. And unless one enjoys this 'communion of sympathy' and its concomitant understanding with regard to matters of the faith, how can it be possible to communicate it? For normally we can communicate only that which we possess. We are faced with a difficulty that admits of no easy solution.

Père Couturier states: 'Every great artist is intuitive. This is almost always enough.'[30] While it is true that any decent artist will possess some degree of intuition with regard to whatever subject matter he is engaging with and while this naturally will be all the more so in the case of great artists, this can never be enough when it comes to matters of faith. One can appreciate the faith only from within. In artistic expression however it is not a question of giving verbal form to one's belief or lack thereof; what is expressed is couched in the conditions of material being according to a pattern of images and motifs which are intelligible to those who inhabit a particular religious tradition. It is sufficient therefore for the artist to point; indeed, that is all he can do, for that is all the material conditions of being allow him to do. While he can perhaps shape the matter of his medium more skillfully than any artist working within the faith, the believer on the other hand will experience a 'communion of sympathy' with the reality to which the artwork points, a communion

30 Père Couturier, in Swiss review *Werk* 4 (1949), 120. Quoted in Régamey, *Religious art*, p. 186.

not open to one outside the faith. The non-believing artist thus can become an instrument of grace for others, facilitating them in experiencing the faith in ways hitherto unknown to them, while he himself remains an outsider to this reality.

The artwork communicates meaning in a way analogous to language. Thus in painting, for example, there is an *iconology*, a pattern of images and motifs in the wider artistic tradition upon which the individual artist can draw. As Nichols tells us, 'Just as a language provides the articulation for the basic set of perceptions available to the people who speak the language, so an iconology forms a possible world of aesthetic perceptions'.[31] Iconology is always culturally conditioned; patterns of images and motifs are necessarily forged in a particular cultural setting. Man is nonetheless a 'culture-transcending-animal' and so in the hands of a great artist a particular iconology has the power to communicate new horizons of meaning 'in a way which transcends that limited cultural setting from which it emerged'.[32] Indeed, as Karl Rahner rightly proclaims: 'In real art the absolutely historical particularity of the artist and the eternal in his proclamation are one.'[33]

Works of art do not simply present a subject matter and please through the arrangement of their parts; they are, as Eldridge points out, 'also made in order somehow to communicate something – an attitude, a point of view, or a feeling about a subject matter'.[34] Any attitude, point of view, or feeling communicated in a work of art does in some sense, as Eldridge rightly states, exist in the maker. In this regard we ought to divest ourselves of the strange idea that artists – writers, painters, musicians, sculptors – have a deep and privileged access to reality, to the meaning of things, and ultimately to truth itself (even if this latter be only the truth that there is no truth!). They too, like the rest of us, have been formed, intellectually and emotionally, in particular cultural contexts as well as undergoing influences which are unique to them as individual

**31** Nichols, *The art of God Incarnate*, p. 94. **32** Ibid., p. 232. **33** Karl Rahner, 'Theology and the arts', *Thought* 57 (1982), quoted in Thiessen, *Theological aesthetics*, p. 222. **34** Eldridge, *Introduction*, p. 68.

human beings. It does not follow therefore that the 'passions and thoughts and feelings' that they experience are 'the general passions and thoughts and feelings of men' as Wordsworth imagined.[35] Eldridge, after allowing that there can be commanding works that bring together many audiences, correctly, in our view, suggests that we perhaps 'need a somewhat more individualistic and pluralized theory of expression'.[36]

The message that an artist communicates is not necessarily one which enriches the inner life of the beholder or, indeed, which conduces to his flourishing as a human being. It can happen that art poisons the inner man, contributes to a distortion of his perception of reality and, in so doing, undermines the conditions of his flourishing. Art actualises its negative potential when in particular it subverts moral values and promotes agnosticism or atheism. When it exercises its power over lives in this way, it can deflect them from answering the call to ultimate beatitude which is at the heart of every human existence. Thus the tragedy of those who genuinely believe in the slogan, 'Art for art's sake'; they are oblivious to the interconnectedness of all aspects of reality. Those who subscribe to this notion are at the very least condemned to lead a schizophrenic existence – and such an existence is by definition unhealthy and undesirable.[37] In the light of what we have said, we must therefore disagree with Aidan Nichols when he suggests that 'Art requires and releases an askesis or discipline of vision so that we learn how to look with a purity of insight into the heart of human life.'[38] By 'purity of insight' Nichols presumably means undefiled understanding that sees things in their objective reality, but we have seen how in fact art has in its power not only to purify but also to sully the life of mind. Nevertheless, Nichols is correct – although his sense ought to be read both negatively as well as positively – when he writes that 'Such looking shifts our whole way of reading the significance of the

---

**35** William Wordsworth, 'Preface to Lyrical Ballads', in *Selected poems and prefaces*, ed. Jack Stillinger (Boston, 1965), p. 447. Quoted in Eldridge, *Introduction*, p. 69. **36** Eldridge, *Introduction*, p. 79. **37** The classic treatment of the fragmentation and compartmentalisation of the various facets of human existence in contemporary society is of course to be found in Alascair MacIntyre, *After virtue: a study in moral theory* (London, 1985). **38** Nichols, *The art of God Incarnate*, p. 100.

world. In its wake we find our own existence reshaped from the experience of what we have seen.'[39]

To the extent that an artwork promotes immoral values, it fails to be ordered toward the Final End of all existence, namely God. This failure detracts from the goodness of the work and therefore also from its beauty, for the meaning which is embodied in its sensuous form lacks due ordering to the Origin and End of all created things. In other words, it is out of sink with the objective order of things as pre-existing in the Divine Ideas and as determined by the Eternal Law. This idea finds textual support in Aquinas in a passage where he discusses the twofold perfection of things. The first perfection concerns the substance of a thing; it is the form of the whole, which arises from the integrity of its parts. The second perfection concerns the end; 'but the end is either the action, as the end of the zitherist is to play the zither, or it is something arrived at by the action, as the house is the end of the builder which he makes by building'.[40] The first perfection is however the cause of the second, because form is the principle of action. Speaking of the ultimate perfection which is the end of the whole universe, Aquinas tells us that this consists in the perfect happiness or beatitude of the saints which will take place at the consummation of time. While Aquinas is here talking about the perfection of the universe as a whole, his comments can just as well be applied to the individual substances which go to make up the whole universe, for 'in a whole the good is integrity, which is the result of the order and composition of parts'.[41]

Appeal to MacIntyre's masterful demonstration that there exist incommensurable traditions of rationality lends support to our contention that there are different and incommensurable conceptions of art. Different conceptions of art in their concrete embodiment in artistic artefacts communicate different – and often irreconcilable – conceptions of the logic of existence. This point is perhaps most forcefully exemplified in the varying opinions about the relationship between art and moral-

**39** Ibid. **40** ST, I,73, I. Translation by Oliva Blanchette, *The perfection of the universe according to Aquinas: a teleological cosmology* (University Park, PA, 1992), p. 105. **41** SCG, 3, 94 [II].

ity. In the Thomistic view of things, there can be no divorce between these two domains of human experience. This position is ultimately grounded in the status of truth and goodness as transcendental properties of being and of beauty, which is the true experienced as good – as coterminous with them.

# CHAPTER SEVEN

# The problem of objectivity

I F IT IS TRUE THAT there are different traditions of rationality and if reason is crucially central to aesthetic perception, then it ought not to be surprising if different conceptions of beauty arise, for beauty is in part a function of reason: *pulchra enim dicuntur quae visa placent.* How can one judge between these different conceptions and the kind of art in which they issue? Does our insistence that there is no such thing as 'pure' reason for Aquinas – although not explicitly signalled, this idea forms an integral part of his thought – not serve to undermine any idea of objectivity in a Thomistic account of aesthetic perception and to cultivate the notion that beauty is in the eye of the beholder? In other words, does our position not commit us to some form of aesthetic relativism?

In brief, the answer to these questions is in the negative. As for Voegelin, the proper connatural context for the unfolding of the life of reason according to Aquinas, is in the 'in-between', that is to say in between the poles of the divine tension. In the philosophical language of Aquinas we might say between the poles of the divine tension of God as efficient cause of all that is – but of the human mind in particular – and of God as final cause.[1] And, of course, these causes are one and the same in the case of God. God is not only the origin of all things; He is also their ultimate goal. In the words of Fran O'Rourke, 'There is ... within creation a circular movement which leads it forth from the original fullness of the source and returns it to God as its final fulfilment. There are within creatures two "strains" or tendencies of being: being from God and being towards God.'[2]

---

1 See Kevin E. O'Reilly, 'Efficient and final causality and the human desire for happiness in the *Summa Theologiae* of Thomas Aquinas', *Modern Schoolman* 82 (2004), 33–58, for a more detailed discussion of this idea.   2 Fran O'Rourke, *Pseudo-Dionysius and the metaphysics of Aquinas* (Leiden, 1992), p. 234.

---

If and when man strives to place himself outside this divine tension, the life of mind necessarily becomes distorted and reasoning becomes divorced from the true nature of things. The tragic consequence of life lived outside the divine tension is the treating of limited goods as absolute and living as though there were no such thing as absolute Truth. In contrast to this closure to existence and the sense of meaninglessness to which it gives rise, Aquinas is quite clear that God has created the human soul and imbued it with a structure whereby it necessarily desires that happiness which is ultimately realised in the beatific vision: 'The object of the will, that is the human appetite, is the Good without reserve, just as the object of the mind is the True without reserve. Clearly, then, nothing can satisfy man's will except such goodness, which is found, not in anything created, but in God alone.'[3] Again, given that truth and goodness are intrinsic to the definition of beauty we can say, basing ourselves on the foregoing remarks, that God has inscribed within the human soul a desire for beauty, a desire which will receive its ultimate realisation in the beatific vision.

What we have just stated about the life of mind in the divine tension must be reiterated with much greater force when life in the divine tension is specified by belief in Christ. As Emile Mersch puts it:

> Once a relation with Being itself is elevated and transformed as it is in Christ, one's way of existing is elevated and transformed, and at the same time the activities that have to do with being, the activities of knowing and willing, are transformed and elevated. Through faith and vision, the Christian knows otherwise than the rest of men; and through charity, he wills otherwise.[4]

This transformation and elevation of the will on the part of the Christian explain why he and the unbeliever, as Peter A. Knasniewski puts it, 'stand at odds regarding the meaning and structure of activities as basic and evidently *good* as natural sexual intercourse and the procreation of offspring'.[5]

---

**3** ST, 1–2, 2, 8. **4** Emile Mersch SJ, *The theology of the Mystical Body*, trans. Cyril Vollert SJ (St Louis, 1952), p. 327. **5** Peter A. Knasniewski, '"Divine drunkenness": the secret

We have emphasised that for Aquinas there is no such thing as pure reason; nor indeed is there such a thing as pure will; rather, they mutually inform one another. This means that all knowledge involves love and all love involves knowledge. Consequently, 'If either the intellect or will functions in a defective manner, then the other will necessarily be distorted in its operation'.[6] One could describe the dynamics of the deformation of the life of mind, on account of its unfolding outside the divine tension, as follows:

> [I]f man no longer seeks God as his final end in response to the restless desire for happiness inscribed within his being by God, then his reasoning concerning what constitutes the good life will become blurred. Moreover, if man does not give intellectual assent to the notion of God as first cause, rectitude of will intent on its true final end becomes an impossibility for him. Consequently, all reasoning about the moral life, both practical and theoretical, is rendered problematic.[7]

In brief, both intellect and will are deformed in their operations to the degree that man withdraws from life in the divine tension. In so far as he thus withdraws, his ability to appreciate true beauty is correspondingly undermined. This assertion may well appear to be strange to many but the logic of our presentation leads inexorably to it, for beauty, as a function of truth and goodness, engages the intellect and will. Nevertheless, it is important to be clear about what is not being claimed. We are not stating that non-believers cannot have any experience of beauty; nor, indeed, are we claiming that all believers have a developed capacity for aesthetic experience. What we mean is that, *all other things being equal*, the quality of this experience will necessary differ from believer to unbeliever. The intellect and will play a crucial role in the experience of beauty; it is therefore natural that a radical difference in the quality of the life of intellect and will would lead to a radically dif-

life of Thomistic reason', *Modern Schoolman* 82 (2004), 11. **6** O'Reilly, 'Efficient and final causality', 51. **7** Ibid.

ferent experience of beauty. When it comes to the beauty of art in particular, matters are even more extreme in that, while beauty is intrinsic to the aesthetic fact for Aquinas, as for the ancients and medievals in general, this state of affairs ceases after Kant. Now, whatever has aesthetic value is not necessarily beautiful and whatever is beautiful does not necessarily have aesthetic value. In other words, art and experience thereof no longer necessarily have any consort with beauty – and therefore neither do they necessarily have anything to do with truth and goodness, at least not in so far as truth and goodness are understood in objective terms.

Given the correlation between possession of a healthy mind and the ability to appreciate true beauty, it is only right and fitting that Christians should have an intense interest in art. For art is perhaps the medium *par excellence* by means of which values and, indeed, disvalues of a particular age are distilled and communicated. Values are never neutral and can never be a matter of indifference, for they enter into the very fabric of a civilisation: with its values, moral and religious, a civilisation stands or falls. It behoves Christians therefore to be discerning about the kinds of art that they espouse, for at times artistic creations communicate constellations of values which do anything but support a civilisation built on faith, hope, and charity. Faith, hope, and charity, those theological virtues which animate a Christian from the very core of his being, also constitute his life in meaningfulness. Nichols is therefore right to proclaim that 'The artwork is rightly judged beautiful or, otherwise expressed, itself, if it embodies the meaningful in the sensuous.'[8]

Because of beauty's intrinsic connectedness with truth and goodness, aesthetic experience thereof can reasonably be considered as having some significance for moral formation. Art therefore has morally educative possibilities. Modernity severed the link between the beautiful and the aesthetic, while mass culture has a tendency to aestheticise everything, no matter 'how marginal, banal, or even obscene it may be'.[9] The anthropocentric turn of modernity, moreover, has meant that aestheticism has been favoured over love of beauty and such aestheticism, which now no

8 Nichols, *The art of God Incarnate*, p. 93. 9 Jean Baudrillard, *The transparency of evil: essays on extreme phenomena*, trans. James Benedict (London, 2002), p. 16.

longer simply embraces the ugly but rather seeks to transport us beyond the categories of the beautiful and the ugly, can serve only to undermine the aesthetic vision of Christianity, a vision to which beauty has always been integral. This aestheticism has arguably manifested itself even in some ecclesiastical architecture, music, art and liturgical practice since Vatican II. Indeed, the increasing secularisation of the life of the Church is perhaps at times nowhere signalled so clearly as in these domains. More pertinently, the lack of appreciation on the part of Church authorities of the role that beautiful things can play in facilitating the transmission of Catholic values has arguably unwittingly contributed to the secularisation of the Catholic mindset. While during the pontificate of John Paul II much was achieved with regard to the monumental task of trying to secure the objective moorings of the true and the good in moral philosophy, Tracey Rowland's contention that this work needs to be supplemented with an account of the effect of mass culture on the soul's participation in beauty has a strong ring of truth about it.[10] While Rowland's contention is undeniably correct, it is nonetheless based on a flawed understanding of the transcendental status of beauty in Aquinas' system. It is therefore to the transcendental status of beauty that we now turn our attention.

## Beauty: a transcendental property of being?

In *De Veritate* 1, 1, Aquinas takes up the problem of being and its transcendental properties as follows:

> Now, as Avicenna says, that which the intellect first conceives as, in a way, the most evident, and to which it reduces all its concepts, is being. Consequently, all the other conceptions of the intellect are had by additions to being. But nothing can be added to being as though it were something not included in being – in

10 See Rowland, *Culture and the Thomist tradition: after Vatican II* (London, 2003), p. 78.

the way that a difference is added to genus or an accident to a subject – for every reality is essentially a being.

Being is therefore not a genus, and nothing can be predicated of it in an adjectival sense. However, there are certain properties according to Aquinas which can be added to being in that they express a mode of being or of presence not made explicit by the term *being* (*ens*) itself.

Aquinas further distinguishes between properties which express a particular or partial mode of the being of being, namely the categories, and properties which apply to every being whatsoever. This is because the mode which the latter express 'is one that is common, and consequent upon every being'.[11] The term 'transcendental' or 'transcendental property of being' is applied to this second kind of attribute in Scholastic philosophy because these attributes transcend all the categories: being can be predicated of each category but no category is predicated of being.

Jan A. Aertsen draws our attention to three points in Aquinas' exposition which are pertinent to our consideration of the status of the beautiful.[12] In the first place Aquinas places the doctrine of the transcendentals within a certain ontological perspective, positing that our concepts must be reduced to 'first', immediate insights. This first insight is being. This point may seem obvious, but its import will become evident as we continue. Aquinas does not offer any argument here for this priority. He does do so however in *Summa Theologiae* I, 5, 2, where he asks which is prior in concept (*secundum rationem*), the good or being.[13] There he also asserts that the first thing conceived by the intellect is being, but adduces a reason: 'In order to be known a thing must actually be.' Thus being is the first intelligible and is prior in concept to the good, this priority being based on its actuality.

If being is the first thing known by the intellect, then all other concepts must arise by way of addition to being. How can this be so? For nothing can be added to being that is not itself being; outside of being

11 This expression does not occur in *De veritate* I, 1, but is employed in XXI, 3. 12 Jan A. Aertsen, 'Beauty in the Middle Ages: a forgotten transcendental?' in *Medieval Philosophy and Theology*, I, 68–97 (73–5). 13 ST, I, 5, 2.

there is nothing. Other concepts, however, give expression to a mode of being not brought out by the term 'being' itself. In this sense they can be said to add something to being. The transcendentals make explicit, not some special, categorial mode of being, but a general mode consequent on every being. It thus becomes evident that the doctrine of the transcendentals has an ontological import: each of them gives expression to a general mode of being.

A second point which merits attention concerns the *relational* nature of the transcendentals. Aquinas divides the transcendentals into two groups, since the mode of being expressed by them pertains to every being either in itself (*in se*) or in relation to another being (*in ordine ad aliud*). In the first group we find 'thing' (*res*) and 'one' (*unum*). Within the group of relational transcendentals we encounter a further twofold classification. In the first place, the relation of one being to another can be considered according to their division. This division is expressed by the term 'something' (*aliquid*), which according to Aquinas implies as it were 'some other thing' (*aliud quid*).[14] In the second place, there is a more positive relational mode of being which is based on the 'conformity' (*convenientia*) of one being with another. Such a relation is possible only if something exists whose nature it is to agree with every being. The soul which, as Aristotle said, 'is in a way all existing things',[15] possesses such a nature. The soul possesses both cognitive and appetitive powers. The term 'good' expresses the conformity of being to the appetite, for the good is defined as 'that which all things desire'. The term 'true' expresses the conformity of being to the intellect, for all knowing is produced by an assimilation of the knower to the thing known, so that assimilation is said to be the cause of knowledge. In the relational transcendentals, the true and the good, the special place of the spiritual being among all other beings is recognised. The human soul is unique in this world in that it is the only being which can conform with every other being.[16]

---

14 See Philipp W. Rosemann, *Omne ens est aliquid: Introduction à la lecture du 'système' philosophique de saint Thomas d'Aquin* for a recent discussion of this transcendental. 15 *De anima*, III, 8, 431b21. 16 Mark D. Jordan comments that 'the irreducible list of "transcendentals" would be *unum*, *bonum*, and *verum*, and that this triplet could be justified

Thus, we might say that humankind is characterised by a 'transcendental openness'.[17] Aquinas displays a certain anthropocentrism in his treatment of the transcendentals.

The third point to which Aertsen adverts is really a simple observation. In *De Veritate* 1, 1, Aquinas names six transcendentals: *ens, res, unum, aliquid, verum, bonum*. In 21, 1, he mentions only four; *res* and *aliquid* are omitted. In neither of the two texts, however, does he assert that beauty is a transcendental.[18] This observation raises some questions. If Aquinas considers beauty to be a transcendental as some modern scholars maintain, why does he not mention it? If the beautiful is a transcendental, what place ought we to assign it in a systematic enumeration of the transcendentals? If it is not a transcendental, what is the nature of its relation, if any, with the transcendentals?

Truncating, but in no way distorting, Aertsen's discussion, we can point out that even by the time he writes the *Summa Theologiae*, Aquinas obviously does not consider beauty to be a transcendental property of being. In the *Summa Theologiae*, he discusses the good (1, 5–6), the one (1, 11) and the true (1, 16). Nowhere, however, does he devote a separate *quaestio* to the beautiful.[19] In fact there are only two texts in the whole of the *Summa* in which Aquinas comments upon the status of the beautiful. It is noteworthy that in both cases beauty is considered only in

by appealing to the basic distinction between *ens* considered in itself and *ens* considered as ordered to another (*in ordine ad aliud*) where the other was either an intelligence or a will': 'The evidence of the transcendentals and the place of beauty in Thomas Aquinas', *International Philosophical Quarterly*, 29 (1989), 393–407 at p. 393. From the evidence we have presented, this is partly true and partly false. The transcendentals can indeed be divided according to 'the basic distinction between *ens* considered in itself and *ens* considered as ordered to another'. However, the relational transcendentals include more than those that relate to either an intelligence or a will. We have drawn attention to those relational transcendentals that can be considered according to their division.   **17** Jan A. Aertsen, 'Beauty in the Middle Ages: a forgotten transcendental?', p. 75.   **18** The only place where the beautiful is encountered in *De Veritate* is 22, 1 ad 12, where it is subsumed under the notion of the good: 'By the very fact of tending to good a thing at the same time tends to the beautiful and to peace. It tends to the beautiful inasmuch as it is proportioned and specified in itself. These notes are included in the essential character of the good ... Whoever tends to the good, then, by that very fact tends to the beautiful.' **19** This in itself is not evidence that Aquinas did not consider the beautiful to be a transcendental for he does not discuss the other acknowledged transcendentals here either.

objections, not in the main body of the article, and that the context of the discussion is always the good.

In ST, 1, 5, 4, Aquinas asks 'whether the good has the character of a final cause'. In the first objection he refers to the opening of Dionysius' treatment of beauty in *De Divinis Nominibus*: 'The good is praised as beautiful.' Since the beautiful has the character of a formal cause, so also must the good. In responding to this objection, Aquinas first of all emphasises the real identity of the beautiful and the good: they are identical in the subject because they are founded on the same reality, namely form. However, they differ conceptually (*ratione*). The good relates to the appetite, for the good is what all things desire; it therefore possesses the character of an end. The beautiful on the other hand relates to the cognitive power. Aquinas then offers his definition of the beautiful: 'For those things are called beautiful which please when they are seen' (*pulchra enim dicuntur quae visa placent*). Since cognition comes about through assimilation, and likeness (*similitudo*) pertains to form, the beautiful properly belongs to the notion of a formal cause.

Elsewhere (1–2, 27, 1) Aquinas inquires 'whether the good is the only cause of love'. In the third objection he quotes Dionysius' statement, found in chapter four of *De Divinis Nominibus*, that the beautiful as well as the good is lovable to all things. It seems therefore that the good is not the only cause of love. Responding to this objection, Aquinas once again draws attention to the conceptual difference between the good and the beautiful. Whereas the *ratio* of the good is 'that in which the appetite comes to rest' (*quod in eo quietetur appetitus*), it pertains to the notion of the beautiful that the appetite comes to rest in the sight or knowledge of it (*in ejus apsectu seu cognitione*). The beautiful therefore adds to the good an ordering to the cognitive power. Whereas the good refers to that which simply pleases the appetite (*simpliciter complacet appetitui*), the beautiful pertains to that the apprehension of which pleases (*id cujus ipsa apprehensio placet*).

The texts which we have cited from the *Summa Theologiae* serve further to emphasise the position expressed by Aquinas in his commentary on *De Divinis Nominibus* of the Pseudo-Dionysius, namely that the beautiful adds to the good an ordering to the cognitive power. This emphasis on the relation of the beautiful to knowledge (*cognitio, visio, aspectus, apprehensio*) constitutes the novelty of medieval thought when compared to Greek thought. However, the transcendental status of the beautiful cannot be ascertained with any degree of certitude from these texts.

For Eco, however, 'these two passages seem definitive, though only implicitly so. They are definitive because … they establish that beauty is a constant property of all being … That is, beauty is identified with being simply as being.'[20] The two texts, however, certainly do not offer a 'definitive' basis for such a conclusion. Aquinas does not identify the beautiful with being, but rather with the good. Aertsen rightly concludes that 'Thomas' formulations suggest … that the beautiful is a specification of the good: the good is that which *simply* pleases, the beautiful is that of which the *apprehension* pleases.'[21]

It might be objected that since the beautiful is convertible with the good and the good is convertible with being, it follows that the beautiful is convertible with being. Beauty is therefore a transcendental. Against this, however, it must be pointed out that the beautiful is not a transcendental *per se*, but achieves a transcendental status, such as it is, only by way of the transcendentality of the good. We might therefore accord a transcendental status to the beautiful in a derivative or secondary sense; however, we ought not to confuse this with the kind of transcendental status accorded to truth and to goodness. The transcendentals make explicit a general mode of being consequent on every being (*modus generalis consequens omne ens*), not a general mode of being consequent on a general mode of being consequent on every being. The beautiful therefore cannot strictly speaking be considered a transcendental.

Our conclusion that beauty cannot be regarded as a transcendental in Aquinas' doctrine seems to be confirmed by the fact that there is an *ordo* of the transcendentals: being is first, next comes the one, then the true and finally the good.

**20** Eco, *Aesthetics*, pp 36–7. **21** 'Beauty in the Middle Ages: a forgotten transcendental', 86.

> Thus the character of the good includes more notes than that of the true and is constituted by a sort of addition to the character of the true. Thus good presupposes the true, but the true in turn presupposes the one, since the notion of the true is fulfilled by an apprehension on the part of the intellect, and a thing is intelligible in so far as it is one; for whoever does not understand a unit understands nothing, as the Philosopher says. The order of these transcendent names, accordingly, if they are considered in themselves, is as follows: after being comes the one; after the one comes the true; and then after the true comes good.[22]

The transcendentals possess a conceptual order in which the later includes what is earlier. From this point of view there can be no place for a unique transcendental, the beautiful, which would synthesise the other transcendentals.[23]

There is nonetheless an incontrovertible relationship between the beautiful and the two transcendentals, the true and the good, in the texts of Aquinas. In his commentary on Dionysius, as we have seen, he observes that the good and the beautiful are really identical but conceptually different, in that the beautiful adds to the good a relation to the cognitive power. In the two texts which we examined from the *Summa Theologiae*, he briefly elaborates this conceptual difference. The beautiful is not identified with being but with the good. Aquinas' formulations indicate that the beautiful is a specification of the good: whereas the good is that which *simply* pleases, the beautiful is that of which the *apprehension* pleases. In this definition of the beautiful, Aquinas firmly establishes a relation between the beautiful and both the intellect and the will, for

**22** *De Veritate*, 21, 3.   **23** This point refutes the argument adduced by F.J. Kovach in which he states that since intellect and will are rooted in the one soul, 'there is no reason why being could not be referred to these two faculties *jointly* and not separately'. He continues: 'Thus, one may say in accordance with Thomas' mind that being, as considered in its convenientia to the soul's faculties taken separately, is contracted, as to the intellect, into verum; as to the will, into bonum; yet, as considered in its convenientia to the soul's faculties taken conjointly, being is contracted, as to the intellect and the will, into pulchrum': 'The transcendentality of beauty in Thomas Aquinas', in *Miscellanea Medievalia 2: Die Metaphysik im Mittelalter*, ed. P. Wilpert (Berlin, 1963), pp 386–92 at p. 391.

*apprehensio* or *visio* pertains to the intellect, while that which pleases relates to the will. Since the object of the intellect is the true and the object of the will is the good, there is established *ipso facto* a definite relationship between the beautiful and both the true and the good.

Our inquiry has led us to deny the beautiful any place in Aquinas' doctrine of the transcendentals. This position does not accord with the conclusions of many philosophers who have written on the subject. Jacques Maritain argues that the beautiful belongs to the order of the transcendentals, being 'in fact the splendour of all the transcendentals together'.[24] Umberto Eco also believes the beautiful to be a transcendental, as we have seen, albeit implicitly so. He does admit, however, that Aquinas' text is 'filled with uncertainties and hesitations'.[25] Francis J. Kovach is much less reserved and cautious in describing the beautiful as 'the richest, the most noble, and the most comprehensive of all the transcendentals';[26] it is 'the only transcendental that includes all the other transcendentals'.[27] Gilson speaks of the beautiful as a '"neglected" transcendental'.[28] Barrett believes that 'beauty is a transcendental, on a par with goodness and truth, and like them, relative'.[29]

In common with these and with many other writers on the subject, we have emphasised the close relation which Aquinas posits between the beautiful and the two transcendentals, the true and the good. However, on the basis of the evidence surveyed in Aquinas' texts, the beautiful cannot be regarded as the synthesis and unity of all transcendentals. It is, rather, a function of truth and goodness: *pulchra enim dicuntur quae visa placent* (beautiful things are those which when seen please). The beautiful is a function of the delight of the will in the apprehension of truth. In the perception of the beautiful therefore the delight of the will follows intellectual apprehension. Rather than being the 'original unity of the true and the good',[30] the beautiful is the true perceived as good.

---

**24** Maritain, *Art and Scholasticism*, p. 172, n. 63b. **25** Eco, *Aesthetics*, p. 47. **26** Francis, J. Kovach, *Die Ästhetik des Thomas von Aquin* (Berlin and New York, 1961), p. 214; trans. by Jan A. Aertsen, 'Beauty in the Middle Ages: a forgotten transcendental?', p. 72. **27** 'The transcendentality of beauty in Thomas Aquinas,' 392. **28** 'The forgotten transcendental: *Pulchrum*', in *Elements of Christian philosophy* (New York, 1960), pp 159–63. **29** 'The aesthetics of St Thomas re-examined', 123. **30** Winifried Czapiewski, *Das Schöne*

Umberto Eco argues that if beauty is considered to be a transcendental 'it acquires a metaphysical worth, an unchanging objectivity, and an extension which is universal'.[31] The implication here is that beauty possesses no such worth, objectivity or extension if it is not a transcendental. Surely, however, if the beautiful is identical with the good, differing only conceptually on account of its ordering to the cognitive power which relates it to the true, it must share in the metaphysical worth, unchanging objectivity and universal extension of both these transcendentals. It does not require the status of transcendentality in order to acquire these properties. Eco, continuing his line of thought, argues that if beauty is a transcendental then there are two fundamental consequences: 'First, the various determinations of being are affected: the universe acquires a further perfection, and God acquires a new attribute. Beauty, for its part, acquires a concreteness and a quality of necessity, an objectivity and dignity.'[32]

In response to this we must point out that as a function of the true and the good and as coextensive with them, wheresoever they reside there also resides the beautiful. God and the universe are beautiful regardless of the transcendental status of beauty. Furthermore, as a function of truth and of goodness and as coextensive with them, beauty necessarily possesses 'a concreteness and a quality of necessity, an objectivity and dignity'. Thus, the fact that the beautiful is not a transcendental property of being has absolutely no metaphysical or aesthetic ramifications, contrary to Eco's belief.[33]

## *Faith, charity, and the aesthetic* visio

The true and the good are themselves both convertible with being; yet they differ logically from one another. Aquinas argues that since the true concerns knowledge whereas the good concerns the appetite, 'the true

*bei Thomas von Aquin* (Freiburg, 1964); trans. by Jan A. Aertsen, 'Beauty in the Middle Ages: a forgotten transcendental?', p. 131. **31** Eco, *Aesthetics*, p. 22. **32** Ibid. **33** See Eco, *Aesthetics*, p. 22.

must be prior in idea to the good'.[34] He gives two reasons for this assertion. Firstly, the true relates to being itself 'simply and immediately', whereas the good follows from being 'in so far as it is in some way perfect'; for perfection is the ground of desirability. Secondly, the true is prior to the good because 'knowledge naturally precedes appetite'.[35] It is important to realise, however, that 'The will and the intellect mutually include one another: for the intellect understands the will, and the will wills the intellect to understand.'[36] Consequently, things that pertain to the intellect can be an object of the will. It is on this account that Aquinas can say that since the true is a kind of good, 'the good is prior in the order of things desirable';[37] it is not, however, prior absolutely.

The nature of the relationship which we have pointed out as holding between truth, goodness, and beauty means that an increased appreciation of truth and goodness ought to lead to an increased appreciation of beauty and *vice versa*. Aquinas, as a Christian theologian, is aware however that the human ability to perceive truth and goodness is undermined by the effects of original sin. While the mind that operates in what, following Eric Voegelin, we have called the divine tension, can attain to some truths concerning human existence,[38] it fulfils its potential to the optimum degree only when it is immersed in the life of grace.

According to Aquinas, the one whose mind and conduct are conformed to the spirit of the world cannot discern the true good. By contrast, the one whose mind has been renewed by grace enjoys right judgment concerning what is truly good.[39] While we do not need grace in order to know those things that lie within the bounds of natural knowledge, we do need it if we are to know higher things. By grace the nature

**34** ST, 1, 16, 4. **35** Ibid. **36** ST, 16, 4 ad 1. **37** Ibid. **38** See Eric Voegelin, 'Reason: the classic experience', in *Anamnesis*, trans. Gerhart Niemeyer (Columbia, MO, 1978), pp 92–3. **39** *Ad Rom*, XII, 2 (967): 'Just as one whose sense of taste has been spoiled does not enjoy right judgment concerning flavours, but rather sometimes loathes those things which are pleasant and desires those which are loathsome, and the one whose sense of taste is healthy enjoys right judgment concerning flavours, so too the one whose affectivity has been corrupted as it were by being conformed to the things of this world does not enjoy right judgment concerning the good, but he whose affectivity is straight and healthy, his sense having been renewed by grace, enjoys right judgment concerning the good'. My trans.

of the soul is transformed so as to participate in the Divine Nature, 'after a manner of likeness, through a certain regeneration or re-creation',[40] enabling him in his intellective power to participate in the divine knowledge through the virtue of faith and in his power of will to participate in the divine love through the virtue of charity.

Aquinas characterises the theological virtues of faith, hope and charity as infused principles that elevate our natural principles of intellect and will:

> Because such [supernatural] happiness surpasses the capacity of human nature, man's natural principles which enable him to act well according to his capacity do not suffice to direct man to this same happiness. Hence it is necessary for man to receive from God some additional principles, whereby he may be directed to supernatural happiness, even as he is directed to his connatural end, by means of his natural principles, albeit not without Divine assistance. Such like principles are called *theological virtues*.[41]

As Michael S. Sherman puts it, 'Faith elevates the light by which the intellect knows the truth, while charity and hope elevate the will's inclination toward the good as its end.'[42] On account of these virtues the attunement of the soul to Ultimate Truth and, consequently, to particular truths as limited participations therein, is brought to a level unimagined and unimaginable to those who see and feel without the eyes of faith and the heart of charity.

It ought to be pointed out that Aquinas is acutely aware of the ecclesial context of faith. While he did not write a separate treatise on the Church, there is nevertheless an embryonic ecclesiology to be found in his work. Thomas F. O'Meara tells us that the Church is for Aquinas 'the background to sacrament, grace, and life where the Incarnation continues in history after the Ascension of the Risen Christ'.[43] The universal

---

**40** ST, 1–2, 110, 4. **41** ST, 1–2, 62, 1. **42** Michael S. Sherman, *By knowledge and by love: charity and knowledge in the moral theology of St Thomas Aquinas* (Washington, DC, 2005), p. 155. **43** Thomas F. O'Meara OP, 'Theology of the Church', in *The theology of Thomas*

Church is governed by the Holy Spirit: 'If we say: *"In" the Holy Catholic Church*, this must be taken as verified in so far as our faith is directed to the Holy Ghost, Who sanctifies the Church; so that the sense is: *I believe in the Holy Ghost sanctifying the Church.*'[44] The Church therefore cannot err, for the Holy Spirit is the Spirit of truth. It can therefore be argued that the notion of *sentire cum ecclesia*, feeling with the Church, that is to say, being 'connatured' with the mind of the Church, the explicator of Scripture and the receptor and transmitter of Tradition, provides us with the criterion for an objective understanding of reality. As that locus in which grace is imparted to the believer, the Church is at one and the same time the necessary context for the optimal functioning of intellect and will, and therefore for the appreciation of truth and goodness. Consequently, she is also the milieu wherein is provided the conditions for the most exalted experience of beauty possible this side of death.

One who enjoys a life of mind elevated by grace is capable of situating things in their proper place in the order of creation. While conscious of his own position in the hierarchy of being as the horizon and boundary as it were of corporeal and spiritual nature – in other words, while having a sense of the proportion that obtains between the different elements of that creation of which he is a part – he is also conscious of the proportion between his actions and the final end of human existence, namely eternal beatitude. The graced aesthete will, in addition to the foregoing, be able to judge to what extent the values communicated by an artwork are proportioned to the Final End. To the extent that they are suitably proportioned to this end, they can be said to be good. On perceiving the truth of this state of affairs and experiencing this truth as good, the graced aesthete will experience the beauty of the meaning embodied in the artwork. Living and moving in the milieu of faith, hope, and charity connatures him with this meaning and, indeed, provides him with a basis for understanding which is not merely arbitrary. What we have just said of course transports Gadamer's assertion that 'understanding realises its full potential only when the fore-meanings that it begins

*Aquinas*, ed. Rik van Nieuwenhove and Joseph Wawrykow (Notre Dame, IN, 2005). **44** ST, 2–2, 1, 9 ad 5.

with are not arbitrary'[45] into the realm of grace. Here we are dealing with the fore-meanings provided by faith.

On the other hand, works that embody in sensuous form meanings which are at variance with the Christian worldview will repel the graced aesthete to some appropriate degree. Such works may well possess aesthetic worth but cannot be said to be beautiful – bearing in mind that in our own times what has aesthetic value is not necessarily beautiful and that which is beautiful does not necessarily possess aesthetic worth. The Christian aesthete may well be able to appreciate this aesthetic worth, but it would be surprising if he were to experience the object as beautiful, for to do so would require that he be connatured with the worldview and the values which it embodies. He will be able to appreciate the values embodied in this artwork as those of a lower, relatively unredeemed, level of existence, viewing a lower level of existence as it were from a higher one. Indeed, he may well be moved to a deeper realisation of his fortune at being blessed with the gift of faith and to a firmer resolve never to let himself slip into the kind of worldview and attendant disvalues written into the constitution of the artwork.

It is quite possible however that an aesthete who is at one with this worldview, who is in a communion of sympathy with it, will subjectively experience the same artefact as beautiful. In other words, because what he beholds resonates with his own existential constitution, he will take delight in it. Indeed, just as Aristotle maintains that a man's moral constitution determines what ends will appeal to him, so too one could posit that one's worldview will influence profoundly what one subjectively experiences as beautiful as distinct from merely aesthetic. Moreover, just as it is the virtuous man who is the rule and measure of virtuous actions according to Aristotle, so too we can argue that the refined Christian aesthete is the rule and measure of what is truly – that is to say, objectively – beautiful.

Fundamentally constitutive of the refined Christian aesthete being the rule and measure of what is truly beautiful is his ability to situate the

---

45 Gadamer, *Truth and method*, p. 270. Gadamer, of course, has nothing to say about the realm of grace; his philosophy is strictly intra-mundane.

experience in such a way that it corresponds to human destiny as a whole and not simply to the present, fleeting moment; that is to say, proportion and integrity in their fullest sense inform his experience. One who lacks this sense in the presence of an artwork runs the risk, as Richard Viladesau tells us, of putting 'his or her whole capacity for happiness into the objects by which the ego is constituted; hence what is experienced as "good" or "beautiful" on the sensual level becomes an idol, an obstacle to the attainment of the spiritually and "truly" beautiful that transcends the ego'.[46] The worldly aesthete fails to 'see' how the object of delight is proportioned to the ultimate destiny of the cosmos; his ability to 'see' is constrained and undermined by egocentrism and so that experience which issues from the interpenetration of human subject and aesthetic object – *visio in actu est claritas in actu* – is necessarily qualitatively defective. Thus, even when both the Christian and the worldly aesthete delight in the same object – albeit in a qualitatively different manner – this delight assists the former on his journey toward Ultimate Beatitude, whereas the latter allows his attention to come to rest in it. One must not on that account despair for our worldly friend, however, for the fact that the genuinely beautiful object, which for some reason captivates his attention, has hidden in its material constitution meanings pointing in the direction of ultimacy, means that he may in some way unbeknownst to himself be prompted to a spiritual conversion.

Finally, let us refer to the notion of proportion in relation to the challenge which the cross of Christ poses for our conception of beauty. The notion of proportion can be seen to be present, albeit implicitly, in Viladesau's treatment of this challenge. Viladesau asserts that the cross is not a beautiful thing; it is rather 'the symbol of a beautiful *act* – on Jesus' part, as self-giving, and (inseparably) on the part of the Father, in raising Jesus from death'. Understood properly, the beauty of the cross is not that of a self-contained object or event; on the contrary, it is a 'moment in God's *poesis*, an element in the theo-*drama* of salvation, whose significance is therefore incomplete except in the *dénouement* of the narra-

**46** Richard Viladesau, *Theological aesthetics: God in imagination, beauty and art* (Oxford, 1999), p. 189.

tive'.[47] (The fact that the cross is proportioned to the resurrection and to God's salvific plan for humankind explains why, throughout the ages, most Christian pictorial representations of the crucifixion have steered clear of 'photographic' realism; they have, with theological acuity, preferred to treat the cross symbolically, 'making it already the manifestation of glory'.)[48] It is in this *dénouement*, manifest only to eyes enlightened by the light of grace, that the beauty of the poor, the sick, the downtrodden, the outcast – in short, those at the sight of whom purely worldly wisdom recoils – becomes apparent. By grace we can see both ourselves and others in the light of God, He Who is 'the creator, the free giver of existence, of the dynamism to self-transcendence, and of the relational ordering of things to one another and to the whole' as well as being 'the "pleroma," the "locus" of the eschatological communion of all with all.'[49] The ability, imparted by grace, to see as beautiful those whom the world regards as lacking beauty and to give oneself in generous self-giving love for them is to participate in the drama of God's loving, salvific design to His creation. Such acts of loving generosity anticipate the 'eschatological beauty of God's "Kingdom".'[50]

---

**47** Ibid., p. 197. **48** Ibid. Viladesau continues: '[I]n pictorial art, in contrast to narrative, movement is fixed and representation is "complete" and unchanging over time. Hence it can only show the true meaning of the cross by visually combining two "moments," representing the cross in the aura of the resurrection. The representation of the crucifixion by itself is "abstract," from a theological point of view, unless it is seen in this light. In this sense, the representation of the cross in most Christian art is already a kind of "theodicy": it shows evil overcome, transformed into good' (ibid., pp 197–8). **49** Ibid., p. 207. **50** Ibid.

CHAPTER EIGHT

# Conclusion

Eco, in the conclusion to his study of the aesthetics of Aquinas, argues that the latter's aesthetics is 'synchronic' on account of its metaphysical premises. As with medieval thought in general, we encounter in Aquinas' thought 'the synchrony of being in the most general sense: being as the first object of the sciences, being in which there is no development, no becoming, therefore no diachrony'.[1] Comparing Scholasticism and Structuralism, Eco tells us that 'both the Scholastics and the Structuralists engage in inquiries based upon the notion of universals'.[2] Structuralism, we are informed, reaffirms 'an atemporality of the structures of the mind',[3] presumably in the manner in which Eco's Aquinas asserts such an atemporality.

Even if we limit ourselves to Aquinas' understanding of *ratio* as discursive in its nature, we have sufficient grounds to refute Eco's outlandish remarks. *Ratio* enables us to penetrate with increasing exhaustiveness the complex structures of objects – whether they be natural or manmade. Aquinas' *intellectus-ratio* distinction lends itself to an understanding of the nature of aesthetic perception as being discursive or historical in character. Thus, even if we do not venture beyond Aquinas' treatment of the life of mind *per se*, we cannot accept the characterisation of his aesthetics as synchronic.

Our own speculative approach to the issue of aesthetic perception has however called attention to further resources in Aquinas' thought which highlight the fact that not only is his aesthetics not atemporal or synchronic, it has rather an intrinsic historical dimension. While things do indeed have an objective structure which offers itself to human perception, human perception is inescapably conditioned by various fac-

1 Eco, *Aesthetics*, p. 217.  2 Ibid., p. 218.  3 Ibid.

tors, factors which can either enhance or undermine the extent to which it is attuned to the reality of things. While the notion of knowledge through connaturality/inclination engages with the epistemic impact of such factors on the moral agent, we have endeavoured to indicate how it can be extended beyond the realm of the practice of moral virtue to that of aesthetic perception. Just as one recent trend in epistemology has, under the influence of virtue ethics, begun to pay due cognisance to the importance of virtue in securing the foundations of knowledge, so too, it might be suggested, aesthetics ought to consider how a virtue approach might enhance its own deliberations.

Our own reflections in chapters six and seven of this present work constitute a very humble effort in the direction of what one might call a virtue aesthetics. This approach of course inevitably encounters the age-old problem of objectivity. With all due respect to Gadamer, who says that the problem of objectivity only arises if one posits absolute truth,[4] Aquinas would reply that absolute truth nonetheless clearly exists – the metaphysical tradition to which he subscribes and to which he makes an original contribution as well as his proofs for the existence of God offer evidence of the latter's unflinching position with regard to objective truth. While it is true that the history of philosophy vacillates between the extremes of Parmenidean atemporality and Heraclitean flux, Aquinas, following Aristotle, synthesises these extremes. This synthesis is realised, however, not only in his metaphysics but also in his ethics. His philosophy of mind, even when viewed on a purely natural plane, also reflects the dual nature of reality as at once both changing and unchanging. Man however does not experience himself as a *causa sui*, that is, as the author of his own existence; his temporal existence unfolds within the eternity

---

4 Jean Grondin summarises Gadamer's attempt to avoid accusations of relativism as follows: 'Gadamer thinks that we can speak of relativism only if we presuppose absolute truth as a possibility, and it owes nothing to history nor language. The accusation of relativism thus presupposes and defends an absolutist knowledge of the truth. This truth claims an absolute perspective (!) which the hermeneutics of facticity deconstructs, given that the very idea of a *fundamentum inconcussum* proceeds from a denial of temporality. If we abandon this absolutism of truth, the charge of relativism loses its *raison d'être*. On the contrary, we learn to see in the historicity of understanding the working mainspring of truth' (*The philosophy of Gadamer*, trans. Kathryn Plant, Chesham, 2003, pp 12–113).

of God as First Cause of all that exists and as the Final Cause to which all things tend. Aquinas pays due cognisance to this reality in his philosophy of mind, although one must go to his treatise on grace and to his treatment of the theological virtues of faith, hope, and charity to appreciate this fact – something which all too many scholars fail to do. Ultimately, it is to the life of grace which we must appeal if we are to secure the moorings of objectivity in the midst of the undeniable historicity of human experience, not simply within the domain of ethics but also in that of aesthetics.

Finally, we would like to refer to Eco's comparison, in the conclusion to his study of the aesthetics of Aquinas, of the medieval *summa* to a computer. As formal systems, he believes that all medieval *summae* are subject to Gödel's theorem which tells us that 'every formal system has within it a little logical termite which nibbles away at it and spoils its perfect self-sufficiency'.[5] Aquinas' system is in this respect, according to Eco, no different from the other medieval *summae*. Eco points out that since experience of beauty requires knowledge of formal causes and since only God can have an exhaustive knowledge of these, only He can therefore have 'the kind of knowledge of the formal structure of being which permits the perception of it *sub specie pulchri*'.[6] Once response to this argument is that there can be gradations in experience of beauty and that the fact that no human experience of an object is informed by the kind of exhaustive knowledge that God enjoys of it in no way rules out the possibility of some experience or other of beauty. The experience of knowledge through inclination, moreover, when it is informed by grace, enables us to begin to 'see' things more from a divine perspective. We put on the mind of Christ as it were, and so even the reality of Christ crucified does not function as a logical termite on account of it forcing us, as it does, to reevaluate our aesthetic commitments. For in so far as we put on the mind of Christ, our aesthetic commitments draw closer to the *visio divina*.

---

5 Eco, *Aesthetics*, p. 202.  6 Ibid., p. 203.

# Bibliography

## LATIN EDITIONS OF AQUINAS' WORKS

*Summa Theologiae*, edited by Blackfriars. London: Eyre & Spottiswoode, 1964–81.

*Liber de veritate Catholicae fidei contra errores infidelium, qui dicitur Summa contra gentiles*, vols 1–3, edited by Petrus Marc, Ceslau Pera and Petrus Caramello. Rome: Marietti, 1961–7.

*Quaestiones disputatae de veritate*, edited by Raymundi Spiazzi. Rome: Marietti, 1949.

*In Aristotelis Librum De Anima*, edited by P.F. Angeli M. Pirotta. Rome: Marietti, 1948.

*Scriptum super libros Sententiarum*, edited by R.P. Mandonnet. Paris: P. Lethielleux, 1929–47.

*Quaestiones disputatae de malo*, in *Opera Omnia* (Leonine), vol. 23. Rome: Commissio Leonina, 1982.

*Quaestiones disputatae*, vol. 2, edited by P. Bazzi and others. Rome: Marietti, 1965.

*De ente et essentia*, in *Opera Omnia* (Leonine), vol. 43. Rome: Editori di San Tommaso, 1976.

*De principiis naturae*, in *Opera Omnia* (Leonine), vol. 43. Rome: Editori di San Tommaso, 1976.

*In librum Beati Dionysii de Divinis Nominibus*, edited by Ceslau Pera. Rome: Marietti, 1959.

*Perihermenias seu de Interpretatione*, in *In Aristotelis Stagiritae*, vol. 1. Parmae: P. Fiaccadori, 1865.

*In Aristotelis libros peri hermeneias et posteriorum analyticorum exposition*, edited by Raymundi M. Spiazzi. Marietti, 1964.

*Super Boetium De Trinitate*, in *Opera Omnia* (Leonine), vol. 13. Rome: Commissio Leonina, 1992.

*In Matthaeum et Joannem opera Evangelistas*, in *Opera Omnia*, vol. 10. Parmae: P Fiaccadori, 1860.

*Expositio in omnes S. Pauli epistolas*, in *Opera Omnia*, vol. 13. Parmae: P. Fiaccadori, 1862.

*In psalmos David exposition*, in *Opera Omnia*, vol. 14. Parma: P. Fiaccadori, 1863.

*Super Evangelium S. Ioannis Lectura*, edited by P. Raphaelis Cai. Rome: Marietti, 1952.

*In Aristotelis libros De caelo et mundo, De generatione et corruptione, Meteorologium expositio*, edited by P. Fr Raymundi Spiazzi OP. Rome: Marietti.

# Bibliography

*In octos libros physicorum Aristotelis expositio*, edited by P.M. Maggiòlo OP. Rome: Marietti, 1965.

*Oposcula Theologica*, vol. 2., edited by Raymundi M. Spiazzi. Rome: Marietti, 1954.

*S. Thomae Aquinatis Opera Omnia*, ed. Leonia, vol. 6. Rome: Polyglotta, 1891.

*Thomae Aquinatis Opera Omnia*, vol. 7, *Aliorum medii aevi auctorum scripta 61*, edited by Roberto Busa SI. Milan: Hamilcaris, 1980.

### ENGLISH TRANSLATIONS OF AQUINAS' WORKS

*Summa contra Gentiles*. Notre Dame: University of Notre Dame Press, 1975:
— *Book One: God*, trans. Anton C. Pegis.
— *Book Two: Creation*, trans. James F. Anderson.
— *Book Three: Providence*, trans. by Vernon J. Bourke.
— *Book Four: Salvation*, trans. by Charles J. O'Neill .

*Treatise on the Virtues*, trans. John A. Oesterle. Notre Dame: University of Notre Dame, 1984.

*Commentary on the Nicomachean Ethics*, 2 vols, trans. C.I. Litzinger OP. Chicago: Henry Regnery, 1964.

*Commentary on Aristotle's De Anima*, trans. by Kenelm Foster OP, and Silvester Humphries OP. Indiana: Dumb Ox Books, 1951.

*Commentary on the Posterior Analytics of Aristotle*, trans. by F.R. Larcher OP. New York: Magi Books, 1970.

*On the Power of God*, 3 vols, trans. English Dominican Fathers. London: Burns Oates and Washbourne, 1932–4.

*Commentary on Aristotle's Metaphysics*, trans. John P. Rowan. Notre Dame, IN: Dumb Ox Books, 1995.

*Commentary on the Gospel of Saint John*, vol. 1, trans. by James A. Weisheipl OP, and Fabian R. Larcher OP. New York: Magi Books, 1980.

*On Being and Essence*, trans. Armand Maurer CSB. Toronto: The Pontifical Institute of Mediaeval Studies, 1968.

*On Charity*, trans. Lottie H. Kendzierski. Milwaukee: Marquette University Press, 1984.

*On Evil*, trans. Jean T. Oesterle. Notre Dame: University of Notre Dame Press, 1995.

### WORKS BY OTHER ANCIENT AND MEDIEVAL AUTHORS

Albertus Magnus, *Commentarii in I Sententiarum*, in *Opera Omnia*, vol. 36, ed. Steph. Caes. Aug. Borgnet. Paris: Vivès, 1893.

—, *De Pulchro et Bono*, in St Thomas Aquinas, *Opera Omnia*, vol. 7, ed. Robert Busa.

# Bibliography

—, *Summa Theologiae Pars Prima*, in *Opera Omnia*, vol. 31, ed. Steph. Caes. Aug. Borgnet. Paris: Vivés, 1895.

Aristotle, *The Nicomachean Ethics*, trans. David Ross. Oxford: OUP, 1987.

—, *Metaphysics*, trans. Hippocrates G. Apostle. Des Moines, IA: The Peripatetic Press, 1979.

—, *De Anima, Books II, III*, trans. D.W. Hamlyn. Oxford: OUP, 1974.

—, *Physics I, II*, trans. W. Charlton. Oxford: Clarendon Press, 1970.

Dionysius the Areopagite (Pseudo-Dionysius), *De Divinis Nominibus*, in *Patralogia Graeca*, vol. 3. Paris: J.-P. Migne, 1857. Translated by Colm Luibhéid as *The Divine Names*, in *Pseudo-Dionysius: The Complete Works*. London: SPCK, 1987.

John of St Thomas, *Cursus Theologicus*, vol. 6. Paris: Vivès, 1885.

Plato, *The Republic*, trans. Desmond Lee. London: Penguin Books, 1987.

—, *Symposium*, trans. Walter Hamilton. London: Penguin, 1951.

SECONDARY SOURCES

Aertsen, Jan, *Nature and Creature: Thomas Aquinas' Way of Thought*. New York: E.J.Brill, 1988.

—, 'Beauty in the Middle Ages: A Forgotten Transcendental?' in *Medieval Philosophy and Theology*, vol. 1. Notre Dame: University of Notre Dame Press, 1991.

Allers, Rudolph, 'The Cognitive Aspect of the Emotions.' *The Thomist* 4 (1942): 589–648.

Arnheim, Rudolph, *New Essays on the Psychology of Art*. Berkeley: University of California Press, 1986.

Barad, Judith, 'Aquinas on the Role of Emotion in Moral Judgement and Activity.' *The Thomist* 55 (1991): 397–413.

Barrett, Cyril, 'The Aesthetics of St Thomas Re-examined.' *Philosophical Studies* 12 (1963): 107–24.

—, 'Medieval Art Criticism.' *British Journal of Aesthetics* 5 (1965): 25–36.

Baudrillard, Jean, *The Transparency of Evil: Essays on Extreme Phenomena*, trans. James Benedict. London: Verso, 2002.

Bosanquet, Bernard, *A History of Aesthetics*. London: George Allen and Unwin, 1904.

Bredin, Hugh, 'The Theory of Beauty,' in *Philosophy and Totality*, ed. J. McEvoy. Belfast: The Queen's University of Belfast, 1977.

—, and Liberato Santoro-Brienza, *Philosophies of Art and Beauty: Introducing Aesthetics*. Edinburgh: Edinburgh University Press, 2000.

Caldera, Rafael-Tomás, *Le jugement par inclination chez Saint Thomas d'Aquin*. Paris: Vrin, 1980.

Callahan, L., *A Theory of Aesthetics according to the Principles of St Thomas of Aquino*. Washington: CUA, 1927.

Camporeale, Ignazio OP, 'La conoscenza affetiva nel pensiero di S. Tommaso.' *Sapienza* 12 (1959): 237–271.

Ceriani, G., 'La gnoseologia e l'intuizione artisticia.' *Rivista di Filosofia Neoscolastica* 26 (1934): 285–300.

Cessario, Romanus OP, *The Moral Virtues and Theological Ethics*. Notre Dame: University of Notre Dame Press, 1991.

Chalmeta, G., 'Intuición estética e intuición ética en Jacques Maritain.' *Anuario Filosófico* 20 (1987): 139–47.

Chenu, M.-D., *Introduction à l'étude de Saint Thomas d'Aquin*. Paris: Vrin, 1950.

Clarke, W. Norris SJ, 'What Cannot Be Said in St Thomas' Essence-Existence Doctrine.' *New Scholasticism* 48 (1974): 19–39.

Coffey, P., *Ontology or the Theory of Being*. London: Longmans, Green and Co., 1914.

Conley, Kieran OSB, *A Theology of Wisdom: A Study in St Thomas*. Dubuque, IA: Priory Press, 1963.

Cottier, Georges. 'La rectitude et la vérité.' *Nova et Vetera* 1 (1997): 19–34.

Curtius, E.R., *European Literature and the Latin Middle Ages*. Translated by Willard R. Trask. London: Routledge and Kegan Paul, 1953.

Czapiewski, Winifried, *Das Schöne bei Thomas von Aquin*. Freiburg: Herder, 1964.

De Bruyne, Edgar, *Esquisse d'une philosophie de l'art*. Brussels: A. Dewit, 1930.

—, *Études d'esthétiqe médiévale*, vol. 3. Bruges: de Tempel, 1946.

—, *L'esthétique du moyen âge*. Louvain: Institut supérieur de philosophie, 1947.

—, 'Du rôle de l'intelligence dans l'activité esthétique,' in *Philosophia Perennis*, ed. F.-J. von Rintelen. Regensburg: J. Habbel, 1930. 1049–59.

Dedek, John F., '*Quasi experimentalis cognitio*: A Historical Approach to the Meaning of St Thomas.' *Theological Studies* 22 (1961): 357–90.

De Wulf, Maurice, *Art et Beauté*. Louvain: E. Warny, 1943.

—, *Medieval Philosophy*. Cambridge: Harvard University Press, 1922.

Eco, Umberto, *The Aesthetics of Thomas Aquinas*, trans. Hugh Bredin. Cambridge, MA: Harvard University Press, 1988. Originally published as *Il problema estetico in Tommaso d'Aquino* (Milan: Valentino Bompiani, 1970).

—, *La definizione dell'arte*. Milan: Garzanti, 1968.

—, *Art and Beauty in the Middle Ages*. Translated by Hugh Bredin. New Haven: Yale University Press, 1986).

Eldridge, Richard, *An Introduction to the Philosophy of Art*. Cambridge: CUP, 2003.

Febrer, M., *Filosofía de la belleza y del arte*. Barcelona: Instituto de Teología y del Humanismo, 1993.

Follon, J., and J. McEvoy, eds., *Finalité et intentionnalité: doctrine thomiste et perspectives modernes*. Paris: Vrin, 1992.

Forest, A., 'Connaissance et Amour.' *Revue Thomiste* 48 (1948), 113–22.

Gadamer, Hans–Georg, *Truth and Method*. London: Continuum, 2004.

Garceau, Benoît, *Judicium. Vocabulaire, sources, doctrine de Saint Thomas d'Aquin*. Paris: Vrin, 1968.

Gardeil, H.-D., *Notes et appendices à La Charité, t. III, Saint Thomas d'Aquin, Somme théologique, II–II, q. 34–46*. Paris: Descleé, 1957.

Geiger, L.-B., *Le problème de l'amour chez saint Thomas d'Aquin*. Paris: Vrin, 1952.

—, 'Morality according to Saint Thomas and Depth Psychology.' *Philosophy Today* 6 (1962): 227–238.

Gerhard, William A., 'Instinctive Estimation of Practical Values.' *The Thomist* 8 (1945): 185– 232.

Gilby, T., *Poetic Experience: An Introduction to Thomistic Aesthetics*. New York: 1934.

Gilson, Étienne, *Painting and Reality*. London: Routledge and Kegan Paul, 1957.

—, *The Arts of the Beautiful*. New York: Charles Scribner's, 1965.

—, *The Philosophy of St Thomas Aquinas*. New York: Dorset Press, 1929.

—, *Elements of Christian Philosophy*. New York: Doubleday, 1960.

—, *The Spirit of Medieval Philosophy*. London: Sheed and Ward, 1950.

—, *History of Christian Philosophy in the Middle Ages*. London: Sheed and Ward, 1955.

—, *Wisdom and Love in St Thomas Aquinas*. Milwaukee: Marquette University Press, 1951.

—, 'Art et métaphysique'. *Revue de métaphysiqe et de morale* 23 (1916): 243–67.

Gracia, J.J.E., 'Critical Study. Medieval Philosophy and the Transcedentals: Aertsen's Characterisation of Medieval Thought and Thomistic Metaphysics'. *Recherches de Théologie et Philosophie médiévales* 64 (1997): 455–63.

Grondin, Jean, *The Philosophy of Gadamer*, trans. Kathryn Plant. Chesham: Acumen, 2003.

Hanke, John W., *Maritain's Ontology of the Work of Art*. The Hague: Nijhoff, 1973.

Hoenen, Peter, *Reality and Judgement according to St Thomas*, trans. Henry F. Tiblier. Chicago: Regnery, 1952.

Janaway, Christopher, 'Kant's Aesthetics and the "Empty Cognitive Stock".' *Philosophical Quarterly* 47 (1997): 459–76.

Jenkins, John I., *Knowledge and Faith in Thomas Aquinas*. Cambridge: CUP, 1997.

—, 'Aquinas on the Veracity of the Intellect.' *Journal of Philosophy* 88 (1991): 623–32.

—, 'Good and the Object of Natural Inclination in St Thomas Aquinas.' *Journal of Medieval Philosophy and Theology* 3 (1993): 62–96.

Jordan, Mark D., 'The Evidence of the Transcendentals and the Place of Beauty in Thomas Aquinas.' *International Philosophical Quarterly* 29 (1989): 393–407.

Kemal, Salim, *Kant's Aesthetic Theory: An Introduction*. New York: St Martin's Press, 1992.

Kenny, Anthony, *Action, Emotion and Will*. London: Routledge and Kegan Paul, 1969.

—, *Aquinas on Mind*. London: Routledge and Kegan Paul, 1963.

—, *Aquinas*. Oxford: OUP, 1980.

Klubertanz, George P., *The Philosophy of Human Nature*. New York: Appleton–Century-Crofts, 1953.

—, 'The Internal Senses in the Process of Cognition.' *Modern Schoolman* 18 (1941): 27–31.

—, 'St Thomas and the Knowledge of the Singular.' *New Scholasticism* 26 (1952): 135–166.

Knight, William, *The Philosophy of the Beautiful*, vol. 1. London: John Murray, 1891.

Kovach, F.J., *Die Ästhetic des Thomas von Aquin*. Berlin: De Gruyter, 1961.

Lalande, André, *Vocabulaire technique et critique de la philosophie*. Paris: Alcan, 1926.

Little, Arthur SJ, *The Nature of Art or The Shield of Pallas*. London: Longmans, 1946.

Lonergan, Bernard, *Verbum: Word and Idea in Aquinas*. London: Darton, Longman and Todd, 1967.

—, *Insight*. London: Longmans, 1963.

—, *Collected Works of Bernard Lonergan: Philosophical and Theological Papers, 1958–1964*, ed. Robert C. Croken, Frederick E. Crowe and Robert M. Doran. Toronto: University of Toronto Press, 1996.

McCabe, Herbert OP, 'Virtue and Truth.' *Irish Theological Quarterly* 62 (1996/7): 161–9.

McClements, Colm, 'The Distinction *Intellectus-Ratio* in the Philosophy of Thomas Aquinas: A Historical and Critical Study.' PhD diss., Université Catholique de Louvain, 1990.

McInerny, Ralph., *Being and Predication: Thomistic Interpretations*. Washington DC: CUA, 1986.

—, *Aquinas on Human Action: A Theory of Practise*. Washington DC: CUA, 1992.

—, *The Question of Christian Ethics*. Washington DC: CUA, 1993.

—, 'On Knowing Natural Law,' in *The Ethics of St Thomas Aquinas*, ed. L.J. Elders and K. Hedwig. Vatican City, 1984. 133–42

MacIntyre, Alasdair, *Whose Justice? Which Rationality?* Notre Dame: University of Notre Dame, 1988.

—, *Three Rival Versions of Moral Enquiry: Encyclopaedia, Genealogy, and Tradition*. Notre Dame: University of Notre Dame, 1990.

—, *First Principles, Final Ends and Contemporary Philosophical Issues*. Milwaukee: Marquette University Press, 1990.

—, *After Virtue: A Study in Moral Theory*. London: Duckworth, 1985.

Mandonnet, R.P., *Opuscula Omnia*. Paris: Lethielleux, 1927.

Maritain, Jacques, *Creative Intuition in Art and Poetry*. New York: Pantheon Books, 1953.

—, *Art and Scholasticism*, trans. J.F. Scanlon. London: Sheed and Ward, 1930.

—, *The Degrees of Knowledge*. London: Geoffrey Bles, The Centenary Press, 1934.

—, *Existence and the Existent*. New York: Vintage Books, 1966.

—, *The Responsibility of the Artist*. New York: Gordian Press, 1972.

—, *The Range of Reason*. London: Geoffrey Bles, 1953.

—, 'On Knowledge through Connaturality.' *Revue Métaphysique* 4 (1951): 473–81.

—, 'De la connaissance poétique.' *Revue Thomiste* 44 (1938): 87–98.

—, 'Signe et Symbole.' *Revue Thomiste* 29 (1938): 299–320.

Maurer, Armand A., *About Beauty: A Thomistic Interpretation*. Texas: Center for

Thomistic Studies, University of St Thomas, 1983.

Mercier, D., *Métaphysique Générale ou Ontologie*. Louvain: Institut supérieur de philosophie, 1910.

Miller, Barry., *The Range of Intellect*. London: Geoffrey Chapman, 1961.

Mothersill, Mary, *Beauty Restored*. Oxford: Clarendon Press, 1984.

Nichols, Aidan OP, *The Art of God Incarnate, Theology and Image in Christian Tradition*. London: Darton, Longman and Todd, 1980.

Noble, M.-D., 'La connaissance affective.' *Revue des Sciences Philosophiques et Théologiques* 7 (1913): 637–62.

Nussbaum, Martha C., *Upheavals of Thought: The Intelligence of Emotions*. Cambridge: CUP, 2001.

Olgiati, Francesco, *L'anima di San Tommaso*. Milan: Vita e Pensiero, 1923.

—, 'San Tommaso e l'autonomia dell'arte.' *Rivista di Filosofia Neoscolastica* 25 (1933): 450–6.

—, 'La *simplex apprehensio* e l'intuizione artistica.' *Rivista di Filosofia Neoscolastica* 25 (1933): 516–29.

—, 'San Tommaso e l'arte.' *Rivista di Filosofia Neoscolastica* 26 (1934): 90–8.

—, 'L'arte e la tecnica nella filosofia di San Tommaso.' *Rivista di Filosofia Neoscolastica* 26 (1934): 156–65.

—, 'L'arte, l'universale e il giudizio.' *Rivista di Filosofia Neoscolastica*, 27 (1935): 290–300.

O'Neill, Charles J., 'The Notion of Beauty in the Ethics of St Thomas.' *New Scholasticism* 16 (1940): 346–78.

O'Reilly, Kevin E., 'Efficient and Final Causality and the Human Desire for Happiness in the *Summa Theologiae* of Thomas Aquinas,' *Modern Schoolman* 82 (2004), 33–58.

—, 'The Vision of Virtue and Knowledge of the Natural Law,' *Nova et Vetera*, 5 (2007), 41–65.

O'Rourke, Fran, *Pseudo-Dionysius and the Metaphysics of Aquinas*. Leiden: E.J. Brill, 1992.

Pareyson, Luigi, *Estetica: teoria della formatività*. Bologna: Zanichelli, 1960.

Pieper, Josef, *Prudence*, trans. Richard and Clara Winston London: Faber and Faber, 1959.

—, *Only the Lover Sings: Art and Contemplation*. San Francisco: Ignatius, 1990.

—, *'Divine Madness': Plato's Case against Secular Humanism*, trans. Lothar Krauth. San Francisco: Ignatius, 1995.

Pizzorni, Reginaldo M., 'La conoscenza della legge o diritto naturale "per connaturalitatem" o "per inclinationem".' *Apollinaris* 58 (1985): 47–67.

Pope, Stephen J., ed., *The Ethics of Aquinas*. Washington, DC: Georgetown University Press, 2002.

Porter, Jean, *The Recovery of Virtue: The Relevance of Aquinas for Christian Ethics*. Westminster: John Knox Press, 1990.

Prost, Mark P., 'In the Realm of the Senses: Saint Thomas Aquinas on Sensory Love, Desire, and Delight.' *The Thomist* 59 (1995): 47–58.

—, 'Intentionality in Aquinas' Theory of Emotions.' *International Philosophical Quarterly* 31 (1991): 449–60.

Putnam, Mother Caroline Canfield RSCJ, *Beauty in the Pseudo-Denis.* Washington DC: CUA, 1960.

Régamey, Pie Raymond, *Religious Art in the Twentieth Century.* New York: Herder and Herder, 1963.

Roland-Gosselin, M.-D., 'De la connaissance affective.' *Revue des Sciences Philosophiques et Théologiques* 27 (1938): 5–26.

—, 'Peut-on parler d'intuition intellectuelle dans la philosophie thomiste?' in *Philosophia Perennis*, ed. F.-J. von Rintelen. Regensburg: J. Habbel, 1930. 709–30.

Rowland, Tracey, *Culture and the Thomist Tradition: After Vatican II.* London: Routledge, 2003.

Sampaio, Laura Fraga de Almeida, *L'intuition dans la philosophie de Jacques Maritain.* Paris: Vrin, 1963.

Saward, John, *The Beauty of Holiness and the Holiness of Beauty: Art, Sanctity and The Truth of Catholicism.* San Francisco: Ignatius, 1997.

Sherman, Michael S., *By Knowledge and By Love: Charity and Knowledge in the Moral Theology of St Thomas Aquinas.* Washington, DC: CUA, 2005.

Sherman, Nancy, *The Fabric of Character: Aristotle's Theory of Virtue.* Oxford: Clarendon Press, 1989.

Steiner, George, *Real Presences.* London: Faber and Faber, 1989.

Tatarkiewicz, W., *History of Aesthetics*, vol. 2, *Medieval Aesthetics.* The Hague: Mouton, 1970.

Thiessen, Gesa E., ed., *Theological Aesthetics: A Reader.* London: SCM, 2004.

Torrell, Jean-Pierre, *Saint Thomas d'Aquin, maître spirituel.* Fribourg: Éditions Universitaires Fribourg, 1996.

Townsend, Dabney, *An Introduction to Aesthetics.* Oxford: Blackwell, 1997.

van Nieuwenhove, Rik and Joseph Wawrykow, eds., *The Theology of Thomas Aquinas.* Notre Dame: University of Notre Dame Press, 2005.

Verbeke, G. 'Le développement de la connaissance humaine d'après saint Thomas.' *Revue Philosophique de Louvain* 47 (1949): 437–457.

—, 'Man as a 'Frontier' according to Aquinas.' in *Aquinas and Problems of his Time.* Leuven: Leuven University Press, 1976. 195–223.

Viladesau, Richard, *Theological Aesthetics: God in Imagination, Beauty and Art.* Oxford: OUP, 1999.

Voegelin, Eric, *Anamnesis*, trans. Gerhart Niemeyer. Columbia, MO: University of Missouri Press, 1978.

Wollheim, Richard, 'Criticism as Retrieval' in *Art and its Objects.* Cambridge, London, 1980. 185–204.

Zagzebski, Linda, *Virtues of the Mind: An Inquiry into the Nature of Virtue and the Ethical Foundations of Knowledge.* Cambridge: CUP, 1996.

# Index

# Index